NEW DIRECTIONS FOR CHILD DEVELOPMENT

William Damon, *Brown University*
EDITOR-IN-CHIEF

Emotion and Its Regulation in Early Development

Nancy Eisenberg
Arizona State University

Richard A. Fabes
Arizona State University

EDITORS

Number 55, Spring 1992

JOSSEY-BASS PUBLISHERS
San Francisco

EMOTION AND ITS REGULATION IN EARLY DEVELOPMENT
Nancy Eisenberg, Richard A. Fabes (eds.)
New Directions for Child Development, no. 55
William Damon, Editor-in-Chief

LC 85-644581   ISSN 0195-2269   ISBN 1-55542-751-0

NEW DIRECTIONS FOR CHILD DEVELOPMENT is part of The Jossey-Bass Education Series and is published quarterly by Jossey-Bass Publishers (publication number USPS 494-090). Second-class postage paid at San Francisco, California, and at additional mailing offices. POSTMASTER: Send address changes to Jossey-Bass Publishers, 350 Sansome Street, San Francisco, California 94104.

EDITORIAL CORRESPONDENCE should be sent to the Editor-in-Chief, William Damon, Department of Education, Box 1938, Brown University, Providence, Rhode Island 02912.

Cover photograph by Wernher Krutein/PHOTOVAULT © 1990.

Printed on acid-free paper in the United States of America.

CONTENTS

EDITORS' NOTES

Major changes are taking place in the scope and conceptualization of research on emotional development, and the chapters assembled in this volume, *Emotion and Its Regulation in Early Development,* reflect these important changes. For example, the long-standing view that emotions are primarily intrapsychic, maladaptive, and disorganizing processes is being challenged (for example, Frijda, 1986; Hinde, 1985). In line with this challenge, the authors of the chapters in this volume reconceptualize emotions as potentially adaptive in the process of coping with the environment and focus on the interpersonal, relational, and communicational aspects of emotion. Without exception, the contributors take a broad, interpersonally oriented view of children's emotionality, emphasizing the adaptiveness and complexity of emotion-related processes.

Also in line with contemporary thinking is the focus on emotion regulation. As was noted by Campos, Campos, and Barrett (1989), a volume of chapters entirely devoted to emotion regulation would have been unthinkable even ten years earlier. Nonetheless, the current interest in emotion regulation reflects a resurgence; many years ago theorists such as Darwin (1872) were interested in the regulatory aspects of emotion expression.

As was recently noted by Dodge and Garber (1991), the term *emotion regulation* has been used in many ways. In some instances, the term implies the regulation of emotions by an external regulator or by an internal process; in other instances, the term refers to the use of emotion to regulate social interactions (Rothbart and Derryberry, 1981). In addition, researchers have not always differentiated between emotion regulation and self-regulation. Emotion regulation often refers to the management of emotional expressiveness and arousal, including negative affectivity, whereas self-regulation frequently refers to the regulation or control of one's own behavior. This distinction between regulation of emotion and regulation of behavior is reflected in the literature on stress and coping in which two primary modes of coping have been identified: emotion-focused coping (coping strategies designed to modulate and control emotional arousal) and problem-focused coping (coping strategies that address the source of the stress, usually by means of some overt behavior; see Lazarus and Folkman, 1984).

As evident in the chapters in this volume, this distinction is not always clear. Behaviors (for example, behavioral inhibition or shifting of one's attention by means of gaze aversion) often serve to modulate incoming stimuli that cause emotional arousal; however, they also can be used to regulate existing levels of emotion or the expression of emotion and to enhance control of overt behavior (for example, aggression). Moreover, internal cognitive processes such as distraction or planning can be used to reduce emotional arousal, regulate ongoing or future behavior, or change (psychologically, physically, or socially) the context in which the individual is embedded. Thus, emotion, action, and cognition are intimately related and appear to interact in ways that help the organism adapt his or her goals to the environment and modify the environment to fit these goals (Campos, Campos, and Barrett, 1989). By elucidating the relations among emotion, self-regulation, and emotion regulation, we can clarify the associations among emotionality, motivation, cognition, and action (Barrett and Campos, 1987; Kopp, 1989).

A major focus of the authors in this volume is the regulation of negative emotionality. One reason for this focus may be that negative affective states and conditions are unavoidable; children must learn to modulate, tolerate, and endure negative affect to a greater degree than is the case for positive affect. Thus, how children learn to regulate negative affective states and conditions is an important and central process in the development of adaptive coping (Mandler, 1975).

Negative emotionality, however, does not always stem from intrapsychic processes or self-related experiences: often it is vicariously induced by exposure to others' negative states and conditions. Observation of another person who is sad or hurt frequently elicits sadness or sympathy in the viewer (see Eisenberg, 1989). As such, children must learn to deal not only with their own directly induced feelings of distress but also with their reactivity to the distress of others.

All of the chapters in this volume focus on the social nature of emotion and support the view that emotions are frequently embedded in social interactions. This orientation reflects a relatively new view of emotion, one in which emotion is defined as "processes of establishing, maintaining, or disrupting the relations between the person and the internal or external environment, when such relations are significant to the individual" (Campos, Campos, and Barrett, 1989, p. 395). For instance, in Chapter Two, Campos, Kermoian, and Zumbahlen delineate the nature of relational changes in the family system brought about by the onset of self-produced locomotion. Their data suggest that when infants acquire the capacity to move about voluntarily, parents begin to treat their infants in a more mature fashion; for example, their expectations regarding compliance, as well as their willingness to apply sanctions for noncompliance, change with the onset of locomotion. These changes appear to influence the quality and intensity of the expression of affect in both infants and parents.

In Chapter One, Rothbart, Ziaie, and O'Boyle examine the development of attentional control as it relates to infants' susceptibility to distress. The authors argue that changes in social interaction are related to developmental changes in attentional control. Infants appear to spend less time visually orientating to their mothers and begin to shift their attention to foci other than the mothers as they gain increased control over visual attention. In turn, mothers begin to hold their infants differently so that the children can more easily look around. The combination of newly acquired visual control and body positions provides children with additional means to alleviate distress (for example, the children can more easily turn away or distract themselves by focusing on interesting visual stimuli).

In Chapter Three, Kopp examines children's emotion-related responses to parents' requests for compliance. In discussing the relation between children's negativity and resistance to parental demands and changes in these behaviors as a function of the onset of language, Kopp argues, like Campos, Kermoian, and Zumbahlen, that developmental changes affect the child's socioemotional environment. Specifically, the development of language appears to reflect a developmental transformation that enables children to deal more effectively with frustrating stimuli. In turn, parental expectations and socioemotional reactions toward the child also change.

In Chapter Four, Eisenberg, Fabes, Carlo, and Karbon focus on the ways in which vicarious emotional arousal influences children's social behavior and social competence. They suggest that there are considerable individual differences in how children cope with arousal experienced as a consequence of exposure to others' emotional states or circumstances. They further suggest that how children cope with this arousal influences the degree to which they respond in socially appropriate and sensitive ways to others' negative states and conditions. Moreover, the data presented are consistent with the argument that parental practices and behaviors are related to the ways in which children deal with their emotions.

In Chapter Five, Bugental, Cortez, and Blue examine children's internal regulatory and cognitive processes in response to the negative affective expressions of others. Although there is considerable evidence that one's *own* negative affective states are associated with biased and reduced information processing (for example, Bower, 1981), much less is known about changes in information processing as a function of witnessing others' negative affect. Bugental, Cortez, and Blue address this important issue.

Finally, in Chapter Six, Saarni reports the results of an experimental study in which she observed children's attempts to change the sad mood state of an adult confederate. Thus, Saarni focuses on children's social control of others' emotions. Compelling findings are presented regarding the degree to which others' moods affect children and the variety of strategies that children use to alter others' mood states.

In summary, the contributors to this volume all address topics relevant to the study of emotion and regulation. Their approaches are quite different, as are the specific processes studied and the ages of the children included in the studies. As such, this volume constitutes an important source of information on the developmental trajectories of skills related to the regulation of emotion and action. Although many questions remain to be addressed and answered, the chapters here provide methodological and empirical foundations for the study of the complex interplay of children's emotions, social interactions, and social competence.

The chapters in this volume were initially presented in February 1991 at an Arizona State University conference on Emotion, Self-Regulation, and Social Competence, sponsored in part by a grant from the Graduate College of Arizona State University. Partial support for the editors' efforts in organizing this conference and compiling this volume came from a National Science Foundation grant to Nancy Eisenberg and Richard A. Fabes (BNS 88-07784) and Career Development and Research Scientist Development awards to Nancy Eisenberg from the National Institute of Child Health and Development (K04 HD00717) and the National Institute of Mental Health (K02 MH00903-01).

Richard A. Fabes
Nancy Eisenberg
Editors

References

Barrett, K., and Campos, J. J. "Perspectives on Emotional Development. Part 2: A Functionalist Approach to Emotions." In J. Osofsky (ed.), *Handbook of Infant Development.* New York: Wiley, 1987.

Bower, G. "Mood and Memory." *American Psychologist,* 1981, *36,* 129–148.

Campos, J. J., Campos, R. G., and Barrett, K. C. "Emergent Themes in the Study of Emotional Development and Emotion Regulation." *Developmental Psychology,* 1989, *25,* 394–402.

Darwin, C. *The Expression of Emotions in Man and Animals.* London: John Murray, 1872 (New York: Philosophical Library, 1955).

Dodge, K. A., and Garber, J. "Domains of Emotion Regulation." In J. Garber and K. A. Dodge (eds.), *The Development of Emotion Regulation and Dysregulation.* Cambridge, England: Cambridge University Press, 1991.

Eisenberg, N. *Empathy and Related Emotional Responses.* New Directions for Child Development, no. 44. San Francisco: Jossey-Bass, 1989.

Frijda, N. *The Emotions.* New York: Cambridge University Press, 1986.

Hinde, R. "Was 'the Expression of the Emotion' a Misleading Phrase?" *Animal Behavior,* 1985, *33,* 985–992.

Kopp, C. B. "Regulation of Distress and Negative Emotions: A Developmental View." *Developmental Psychology,* 1989, *25,* 343–354.

Lazarus, R. S., and Folkman, S. *Stress, Appraisal, and Coping.* New York: Springer-Verlag, 1984.

Mandler, G. *Mind and Emotion.* New York: Wiley, 1975.

Rothbart, M. K., and Derryberry, D. "Development of Individual Differences in Temperament." In M. E. Lamb and A. L. Brown (eds.), *Advances in Developmental Psychology.* Vol. 1. Hillsdale, N.J.: Erlbaum, 1981.

RICHARD A. FABES *is associate professor in the Department of Family Resources and Human Development at Arizona State University. His areas of research include social and emotional development, television, and children's intrinsic versus extrinsic behavior.*

NANCY EISENBERG *is Regents' Professor of psychology at Arizona State University. Her research interests include social, emotional, and moral development.*

*Infants' orienting of attention undergoes marked development in
the first six months of life, and changes in attentional control
appear to be related to infants' susceptibility to distress.*

Self-Regulation and Emotion in Infancy

Mary K. Rothbart, Hasan Ziaie, Cherie G. O'Boyle

Our study of individual differences in temperament has led us to an interest
in the interaction between emotion and such self-regulatory processes as
attention (Rothbart, Posner, and Boylan, 1990). We have defined temperament as individual differences in reactivity and self-regulation assumed to
have a constitutional basis, influenced over time by the interaction of
heredity, maturation, and experience (Rothbart, 1989; Rothbart and Derryberry, 1981). The distinction between reactivity and self-regulation is
useful because it allows us to consider individual differences in self-regulatory systems that serve important organizing functions with respect to
motor activity and emotion.

In our studies of self-reported temperament in adults and adolescents
and caregiver-reported temperament in children, we have found that higher
levels of reported attentional control are related to lower susceptibility to
distress (Capaldi and Rothbart, 1990; Derryberry and Rothbart, 1988; Rothbart and Hershey, 1990). We have therefore undertaken a collaboration
between attention and temperament development projects at Oregon in an
effort to illuminate the interaction between self-regulation and emotion
during early development (Rothbart, Posner, and Boylan, 1990). In this
chapter we report on some of the results of this collaborative work and
describe our longitudinal study of self-regulation.

Early Development of Attentional Systems

In our work on the development of attention, we focus on the development
of attentional controls as related to neural development and to the infant's
susceptibility to distress (Johnson, Posner, and Rothbart, 1991). The first

NEW DIRECTIONS FOR CHILD DEVELOPMENT, no. 55, Spring 1992 © Jossey-Bass Publishers attention system we have studied involves orienting of attention toward visual locations (the posterior attention system; see review by Posner and Peterson, 1990). The second (the anterior attention system) involves orienting of attention toward the products of memory systems as well as toward target stimuli. We have suggested that there are important developments in the posterior system during the period from three to six months, and that developments in the anterior system may be observed during the last six months of the first year of life (Posner and Rothbart, in press).

Development of the Posterior System

Infants' orienting of attention in space undergoes marked development between two and six months of life, with changes related to infants' preferences for novel locations (Clohessy, Posner, Rothbart, and Vecera, in press; Rothbart, Posner, and Boylan, 1990), their ability to disengage gaze from an external stimulus (Johnson, Posner, and Rothbart, in press), and their ability to anticipate the location of upcoming visual events (Haith, Hazan, and Goodman, 1988; Johnson, Posner, and Rothbart, in press). Development of infants' ability to disengage attention from one location so as to move it to another and their ability to anticipate the location of future events would appear to be particularly important for the early self-regulation of emotion.

In our research (Johnson, Posner, and Rothbart, 1991) we videotaped thirty-two two-month-olds, twenty-one three-month-olds, and twenty-one four-month-olds as they sat in front of the center color monitor of a three-monitor horizontal display controlled by two personal computers. We studied both contingency learning and disengagement in the infants. A central attractor stimulus, composed of a colored sound-light display, was presented to the infant. On training trials the attractor stimulus was turned off when the infant was judged to be looking at it; after one second a peripheral stimulus then appeared on one of the two side screens (thirty degrees from center). The position of the peripheral stimulus to the right or left of the child was dependent on which of two attractor stimuli (a looming stimulus or a diamond) had been presented on the central display. On test trials, the peripheral stimulus appeared on both the right- and left-hand screens so that we could judge the infants' learning of the location contingency. On disengage trials, the procedure was similar to training trials except that the attractor stayed on after the peripheral stimulus appeared. If the infant had not disengaged gaze from the attractor after eight seconds, we terminated the trial and classified it as a failure to disengage.

In our disengagement measure, we found that four-month-old infants disengaged much more readily than did the younger infants. The four-month-olds, on average, disengaged during nearly 90 percent of the trials, in comparison with 36 percent and 46 percent disengagement rates for two- and three-month-olds, respectively. In our measure of contingency learning, only the four-month-olds showed a significant, above-chance preference for the predicted side (61 percent versus 56 percent for the other two age groups, respectively). Thus, a developmental shift appears to be occurring between three and four months on both of these capacities.

We then asked whether infants' ability to disengage is related to their susceptibility to the negative emotions and to their soothability. Mothers filled out the Infant Behavior Questionnaire (IBQ), a caregiver report measure of infant temperament that assesses the child's tendency to express the negative affects of fear and distress to limitations (frustration) as well as their soothability during the past week or, for some items, during the past two weeks (Rothbart, 1981). We found that the four-month-old infants who were better able to disengage tended to be less susceptible to negative affect (fear $r = -.39$, $p < .10$; distress to limitations $r = -.47$, $p < .05$) and more soothable ($r = .50$; $p < .05$), as described by their mothers. The direction of the relation between contingency learning and our affect measures was the same (the respective r's $= -.22$, $-.34$, and $.42$), but only marginal significance was attained. Although these findings require replication, they are congruent with the notion that the control of visual-spatial orienting and the expression of negative emotion are related by four months of age.

Development of these attentional abilities are in turn related to brain development (Johnson, 1990). Evidence from neuroanatomy indicates that only the deeper layers of the primary visual cortex are supportive of organized activity in the newborn. During the first weeks of life, development of middle-level lamina come to support an inhibitory pathway to the superior colliculus. For a period of several weeks, this control system may inhibit disengagement when the infant is engaged at a visual location. It is likely that this development is also responsible for the phenomenon of "obligatory attention" observed in young infants, where infants look at a single location for extended periods, sometimes appearing to try to move their gaze but not being able to do so, and becoming distressed after a period of intense looking (see review by Posner and Rothbart, 1981). By four months of age, development of parietal cortex (Posner and Peterson, 1990) and/or frontal eye field connections (Johnson, 1990) allows for more flexible disengagement of attention and greater self-regulation by the infant.

These early developments in attentional control are of interest to those who study socioemotional development because early changes in social interaction may be related to these changing patterns of self-regulation. When caregiver and infant are observed interacting with one another in the vis-à-vis position (face to face), periods of extended visual orienting of the infant toward the mother seen at six and thirteen weeks are followed by decreased orienting toward her by six and one-half months (Kaye and Fogel, 1980). In other studies, a shift of infant visual orienting to foci other than the mother has been observed by about four months of age (Cohn and Tronick, 1987; Kaye and Fogel, 1980). This change in infant orienting is often associated with the mother turning the infant away from the vis-à-vis position so that the child can more easily look around.

Several hypotheses have been put forward to explain this developmental shift, including the idea that infants' looking reflects a new ability and interest in differentiating people from objects, and the idea that improvements in visually guided reaching toward objects are followed by increased visual attention toward objects. We suggest that these changes in social interaction may also be related to developmental changes in the functioning of the posterior attention system, especially in the child's increasing ability to disengage from visual locations and to anticipate events at different spatial locations.

Later Developments of Self-Regulation: A Developmental Study

Literature on early development suggests that infants demonstrate their knowledge of the world via visual-spatial orienting before it is demonstrated via other action systems such as reaching and body orientation (Baillargeon, Spelke, and Wasserman, 1985; Schaffer, 1974). These later developments may be related to the development of more general forms of volition associated with the functioning of the anterior attention system (see Posner and Peterson, 1990). We have carried out a longitudinal study (at 3, 6.5, 10, and 13.5 months) in which we have observed the development of behaviors that may serve to regulate distress (Ziaie, 1988). This work is part of a larger longitudinal study of temperament in which infants were presented with auditory, visual, and tactile stimuli varying in novelty, intensity, and complexity, and their reactions videotaped. Because these episodes were designed to evoke emotional reactions, they proved to elicit a number of self-regulatory strategies.

Behaviors that had been identified as self-regulatory in the literature were grouped together into larger functional categories (Rothbart and Derryberry, 1981). The larger categories included *active avoidance* (including specific behaviors of arch back, arm retraction, leave chair, lean away, push back, and withdraw hand), *orientation toward mother* (look toward mother, lean toward mother, and leave chair toward mother), *disengagement of attention* (gaze aversion, look down, look away, turn head, and look toward experimenter), *approach* (lean forward, reach, point reach, and inhibited reach), *attack* (bang toy, pounding, and push toy away), *body self-stimulation* (arm movement, banging, body movement, kicking, and repeated hand movement), *tactile self-soothing* including hand-mouth activity (hand-mouth, mouthing), touch ear-head, and clasp hands, and *respiration* (heavy breathing, sighs, and yawns).

We coded the occurrence of these behaviors and examined their developmental stability and change across the early months, investigated possible gender differences, and assessed stability of individual strategies of self-regulation. We also examined the relationship between self-regulatory behaviors and infant temperament by investigating relationships between self-regulation and infant emotionality at 13.5 months as reported by the mother and observed in the laboratory. We expected that by 13.5 months, the negative emotions of fear and distress to limitations might be differentially related to patterns of self-regulation, with fear related to less active forms of coping, and distress to limitations related to active attack. In addition, we attempted to replicate Escalona's (1968) finding that more active children are less likely to engage in oral self-soothing, and to test whether Korner's (1973) findings of greater oral activity in girls than in boys extend beyond the neonatal period.

We were also interested in the extent to which infants' self-regulative behaviors were related to their overall distress and smiling and laughter in the laboratory; we expected that if self-regulatory techniques were effective, they might limit distress and enhance positive affect. Finally, we attempted to determine whether distress shown at 3 months in the laboratory would be predictive of specific patterns of self-regulation at 13.5 months.

Methods. The general method employed in this study involved the presentation of emotion-eliciting stimuli to infants in the laboratory. Infant reactions were videotaped and later coded with respect to self-regulatory behaviors.

Subjects. Sixty-six subjects, half girls and half boys, were originally recruited through letters and phone calls to parents whose infants' birth announcements were published in the local newspaper. Of these, we collected whole or partial data at all ages (3, 6.5, 10, and 13.5 months) for fifty-nine infants. Subjects represented a broad range of socioeconomic status and reflected the racial homogeneity of the Eugene-Springfield, Oregon, area, that is, primarily Caucasian. Ten subjects were eventually excluded from our self-regulation analysis due to missed sessions and incomplete records. Data from the remaining forty-nine subjects (twenty-nine boys and twenty girls) were used in this study.

Procedures. In the laboratory, infants' affective and motor responses to stimuli varying in novelty, intensity, complexity, and accessibility were videotaped. The taping sessions occurred twice at 3, 6.5, 10, and 13.5 months of age, with the first session scheduled within one week of the designated ages. Within age periods, the two laboratory sessions were scheduled one week apart, with each session lasting approximately thirty to forty-five minutes. Due to the time demands of coding, only the first day's data are considered here.

Infants were placed in an infant seat (at 3 months) or a high chair (at 6.5, 10, and 13.5 months), within a three-sided gray enclosure. Because of restlessness of 13.5-month-old infants in the enclosure, approximately half of the episodes at that age were conducted at a table. For the gray enclosure episodes, the parent (in almost all cases, the mother) was seated in a chair approximately sixty centimeters to the infant's right and watched the session on a television monitor located to the parent's right. For the table episodes, the parent was seated at the table to the infant's left, at about the same distance. The parent was asked to refrain from talking to the infant during the laboratory procedure but to feel free to smile and provide nonverbal reassurance when the infant looked at the parent. Thus, the parent could provide security for the infant without becoming actively involved in stimulus presentations.

Sessions consisted of nineteen episodes for the 3- and 6.5-month-olds, and twenty-one and twenty-five episodes for the 10- and 13.5-month-olds, respectively. The following episodes were employed at 13.5 months, and a subset was used at the younger ages: social (welcoming speech); Simon (tone and light display); bell (rung out of the subject's view); boredom (a period of 30 seconds with no stimuli present); parasol (a rapidly opening paper parasol); masks (bear masks out of reach); Simon; bell; boredom; checkerboards (black-and-white checkerboards out of reach); face (clown's face out of reach); bubbles (baby shampoo bubbles); social (as above); squeeze toys (four-inch doll and two-inch squeezeable porcupine); peek-a-boo; dog (mechanical dog); rattle (out of reach); rattle (within reach); gonna-get-you (social game with experimenter and parent); music box; bell (out of reach); bell (within reach); cup, spoon, and blocks; clapping blocks; duck (mechanical duck); jack-in-the-box; and "wah-wah" noise (made by experimenter). The length of episodes varied from 15 to 180 seconds. All episodes were coded for self-regulatory behaviors except those involving low-intensity stimuli such as the squeeze toys and the rattle and bell.

Coding Procedures. Behavioral codes were developed to assess instances of behavioral approach, avoidance, orientation toward the mother, disengagement of attention, self-stimulation, and self-soothing. These behaviors were coded either by frequency count or by indication of their presence/ absence for each fifteen-second interval. Percentage agreement among coders was computed during training, and once the criterion of 85 percent interrater reliability was achieved on at least three tapes, coders independently coded the remaining tapes, with weekly reliability checks to maintain the agreement level and to discuss any disagreements. Direction of gaze and other motor behaviors were not coded at 3 months because the reliability criterion was not satisfied for that age group. After completion of coding, functionally related behaviors were combined into composite scores.

For frequency data, the rate of occurrence of behaviors per interval was calculated for each episode and averaged across episodes. For composite scores, the frequency of occurrence for all component behaviors was calculated for each episode and averaged over all episodes. For presence/

absence data, the proportion of intervals in which a behavior or composite was present in an episode was averaged over all episodes.

Of the regulatory behaviors identified, look at experimenter was measured only at 13.5 months. All attentional, tactile self-stimulation, and active avoidance variables were assessed in frequency counts only at 6.5, 10, and 13.5 months of age, due to lack of reliability of coding at 3 months. The remaining behaviors were measured at 3, 6.5, 10, and 13.5 months of age using presence/absence information.

At each age the IBQ (Rothbart, 1981) was also administered. The IBQ is a caregiver measure assessing the frequency of occurrence of temperament-related behaviors during the past week or, for some items, two weeks (see review of validity in Goldsmith and Rothbart, 1991). Data from this instrument were analyzed only for the 13.5-month administration for activity level and for fear and distress to limitations. In addition, latency, intensity, and duration measures of overall distress at 3 and 13.5 months and smiling and laughter at 13.5 months were standardized and averaged within each category. The behavioral codes for describing distress and positive affect are described in detail elsewhere (Rothbart, 1988).

Results and Discussion. Two-way, repeated-measures analyses of variance (ANOVAs), across age (6.5, 10, and 13.5 months) and between sex, were computed for each variable. Because many of the variables occurred infrequently (with skewed distributions), subjects' scores were multiplied by a factor of one thousand and then transformed to natural logarithms to satisfy the assumption of homogeneity of variances. Analyses for six regulatory behaviors or composites (*arch back, push back, touch ear, touch ear-head, arm movement 2, overall disengagement of attention*) yielded neither significant main effects nor interactions. For the variables with statistically significant ANOVAs ($p < .05$ F-ratios), Tukey post hoc comparison tests were applied. Table 1.1 presents summarized results of these analyses with means for each variable. Since 135 F-ratios were computed, it was expected, considering familywise error, that 6 F-ratios would reach significance by chance. Overall, 39 significant F-ratios were found.

Regulation Via Social Communication and Attention. Table 1.1 presents changes in the measures related to social communication and attentional mechanisms. An age effect was found for *orientation toward mother* (composite of *leave chair, look,* and *lean toward mother*). Both 10- and 13.5-month-old infants showed more orientation toward mother than did 6.5-month-old infants. All behaviors included in this composite involved attentional refocusing from the stimulus to the mother, but they differed in the extent of the child's associated body movement. In *look toward mother,* the child visually orients toward the mother but shows minimal movement toward her. In *lean toward mother,* the child's body moves in the direction of the mother while the child is looking at her. In *leave chair toward mother,* the child begins to get out of the chair in the mother's direction. All of these behaviors were

Table 1.1. Means for Self-Regulation

Variable	Age				F-Ratio for Age
	3 mos	6.5 mos	10 mos	13.5 mos	
Frequency Measures					
Overall disengagement of attention*	—	2.28	2.47	2.32	n.s.
Orientation toward mother*	—	.40^a	.69^b	.90^b	$F(2,94) = 22.89$
Leave chair toward mother	—	.04^a	.07^b	.07^b	$F(2,94) = 6.29$
Look toward mother	—	.32^a	.48^b	.47^b	$F(2,94) = 10.18$
Lean toward mother	—	.04^a	.15^b	.36^c	$F(2,94) = 96.27$
Disengagement of attention*	—	1.88^a	1.78^a	.84^b	$F(2,94) = 72.98$
Gaze aversion	—	.01^{a,b}	.01^a	.00^b	$F(2,94) = 3.40$
Look down	—	.32^a	.22^a	.07^b	$F(2,94) = 7.50$
Look away	—	1.48^a	1.46^a	.73^b	$F(2,94) = 46.83$
Turn head	—	.08^a	.13^b	.04^a	$F(2,94) = 7.79$
Pointing	.00^a	.00^a	.01^a	.04^b	$F(3,141) = 17.21$
Tactile and body self-stimulation					
Touch ear-head*	—	.07	.13	.05	n.s.
Touch ear	—	.04	.05	.01	n.s.
Touch head	—	.04^b	.08^a	.04^b	$F(2,94) = 4.48$
Presence-Absence Measures					
Hand-mouth*	.80^a	.66^{a,b}	.64^{a,b}	.42^b	$F(3,141) = 6.90$
Hand-mouth 1	.06^a	.04^b	.09^a	.03^b	$F(3,141) = 7.67$
Hand-mouth 2	.14^{a,b}	.15^a	.16^b	.09^a	$F(3,141) = 3.13$
Mouthing	.60^a	.47^b	.38^{b,c}	.30^c	$F(3,141) = 8.81$
Clasp hands	.23^a	.06^b	.11^a	.07^{a,b}	$F(3,141) = 6.69$
Attack*	.01^a	.18^b	.10^b	.22^c	$F(3,141) = 10.88$
Bang toy	.01^a	.13^b	.00^a	.02^a	$F(3,141) = 40.47$
Pounding	.00^a	.03^b	.03^{a,b}	.06^b	$F(3,141) = 4.11$
Push toy away	.00^a	.02^a	.07^b	.14^b	$F(3,141) = 12.41$

Body self-stimulation*	.89[a]	.93[a]	.57[b]	.94[a]	$F_{(3,141)} = 7.83$
Arm movement 1	.00[a]	.03[b]	.03[b]	.03[b]	$F_{(3,141)} = 7.82$
Arm movement 2	.00	.01	.00	.00	n.s.
Banging	.45[a]	.43[a]	.21[b]	.27[b]	$F_{(3,141)} = 7.93$
Body movement	.00[a]	.02[b]	.04[b]	.03[b]	$F_{(3,141)} = 8.14$
Kicking	.34[a]	.32[a]	.11[b]	.55[c]	$F_{(3,141)} = 39.65$
Repeated hand movement	.10[a]	.12[a]	.17[b]	.07[a]	$F_{(3,141)} = 5.91$
Approach and avoidance					
Frequency Measures					
Active avoidance*	—	.30[a]	.29[a,b]	.29[b]	$F_{(2,94)} = 3.62$
Arch back	—	.13	.06	.04	n.s.
Arm retraction	—	.08[a]	.03[a,b]	.01[b]	$F_{(2,94)} = 6.63$
Leave chair	—	.00[a]	.01[b]	.01[a,b]	$F_{(2,94)} = 3.26$
Lean away	—	.05[a]	.10[b]	.14[b]	$F_{(2,94)} = 22.38$
Push back	—	.01[a]	.01[a]	.01[a]	n.s.
Withdraw hand	—	.03[a]	.09[b]	.09[b]	$F_{(2,94)} = 12.50$
Presence-Absence Measures					
Approach*	.09[a]	.42[b,c]	.31[b]	.54[c]	$F_{(3,141)} = 53.16$
Inhibited reach	.00[a]	.06[b]	.05[b]	.09[c]	$F_{(3,141)} = 29.36$
Lean forward	.01[a]	.07[b]	.03[b]	.05[b]	$F_{(3,141)} = 12.43$
Pointing	.00[a]	.00[a]	.01[a]	.04[b]	$F_{(3,141)} = 17.21$
Reach	.08[a]	.29[b]	.22[b]	.37[c]	$F_{(3,141)} = 32.95$
Respiratory system					
Heavy breathing	.69[a]	.44[a]	.10[b]	.18[b]	$F_{(3,141)} = 30.00$
Sighs	.28[a]	.63[b]	.33[a]	.54[b]	$F_{(3,141)} = 18.26$
Yawns	.01[a]	.01[a,b]	.00[a,b]	.00[b]	$F_{(3,141)} = 3.20$

Note: All reported F values are significant at $p < .05$. Asterisks indicate composite measures.

[a,b,c] Matching superscripts indicate no significant differences ($p < .05$) by Tukey test.

at their lowest point at 6.5 months and significantly increased by 10 months. Only *lean toward mother* showed an additional increase between 10 and 13.5 months.

Disengage attention (composite of *gaze aversion, look down, look away,* and *turn head*) assesses the child's change of focus of attention from the stimulus to aspects of the environment other than the mother. This variable decreased from its first assessment at 6.5 months to its assessments at 10 and 13.5 months. Of four specific behaviors composing this variable, *gaze aversion* (a brief glance down and away from the stimulus) occurred rarely, and *look down* (directing gaze downward) and *look away* (directing gaze away from the stimulus but not toward the mother) occurred more frequently and decreased from 6.5 to 10 months and again to 13.5 months. *Turn head* (head is turned ninety degrees away from the stimulus but not in the direction of the mother) increased between 6.5 and 10 months and then decreased to 13.5 months.

Overall disengagement of attention is a higher-order composite measure formed by combining the *disengage attention* and *orientation toward mother* measures with *look toward experimenter* at 13.5 months. The composite, which assessed overall visual orienting of the infants away from the stimulus, showed no developmental change after 6.5 months. Overall visual orienting away from the stimulus did not change across this period, but, as noted above, significant developmental changes *were* found when the object of the change was specified as either the mother or inanimate aspects of the environment. Whereas the behavior of looking from the stimulus to aspects of the environment other than the mother (*disengage attention* variable) significantly decreased across age groups, looking from the stimulus to the mother (*orientation toward mother* variable) increased between 6.5 and 10 and between 6.5 and 13.5 months.

These developmental changes may be related to increasing communication ability in the older infants, and possibly to development of the anterior attention system, allowing children to respond to the memory of their mothers' locations. By 8 to 9 months of age, infants are able to communicate with another person about a third event in the environment, and social referencing is possible (Klinnert, Emde, Butterfield, and Campos, 1983). The infants also are likely to show increasing ability to remember where their mothers are located so as to be able to turn toward them.

Development of the related behavior of *pointing* (extending the arm or arms toward the stimulus with the finger of at least one hand extended in a point) was also found. At 3 months of age none of our subjects showed pointing. At 6.5 months pointing was observed for the first time, and it increased to a peak at 13.5 months of age. Pointing as a communicative ability has been found by others to develop in the second half of the first year (Leung and Rheingold, 1981).

Regulation Via Tactile Self-Stimulation. We first considered self-stimulatory behaviors that are related to soothing. Of these, *touch ear-head* is a composite variable that showed no developmental change. Of the two variables that were the components of this measure, only *touch head* showed developmental change, with 10-month-old infants touching their heads more often than did 6.5- and 13.5-month-olds.

Hand-mouth is a composite measure assessing oral self-soothing. This variable was at its peak at 3 months and gradually decreased to its lowest level at 13.5 months of age. Three specific behaviors composed this measure: *hand-mouth 1* (finger[s], thumb, or hand[s] in contact but not engaged with the mouth or mouth region), *hand-mouth 2* (finger[s] or thumb engaged in mouth), and *mouthing* (movements of tongue and/or lips, including tongue protrusion, lip smacking, and blowing bubbles), all of which decreased to their lowest levels by 13.5 months of age. *Mouthing* decreased across the age range studied, whereas the other two variables fluctuated across the period, with low levels at 6.5 and 13.5 months of age. *Clasp hands* (touching fingers of one hand against the other hand or hand's finger[s]) decreased significantly between 3 and 6.5 months, increased slightly between 6.5 and 10 months, and then decreased between 10 and 13.5 months of age.

We also considered variables that may serve to increase stimulation. *Body self-stimulation* is a composite measure assessing the child's motor movement, which was at its lowest level at 10 months. Six specific behaviors made up this composite. *Arm movement 1* (waving and sweeping of arms with less than twelve-inch extension) and *arm movement 2* (waving and sweeping of arms with twelve or more inches of extension) occurred rarely. *Banging* (hitting the table with the hand) was at its peak at 3 and 6.5 months, decreasing at 10 and 13.5 months. *Body movement* (movement of head or body) occurred rarely but was greater at the three older ages than at 3 months. *Kicking* (moving the legs and banging the feet against the high chair) decreased at 10 months and then peaked at 13.5 months of age. *Repeated hand movement* (repeated scratching of the bumper or table, opening and closing of hand, and finger movements) includes minimal body movements that may indicate tension. This variable was at its highest level at 10 months.

The overall decrease in *body self-stimulation* at 10 months is primarily due to decreases in *banging* and *kicking,* since these two variables are the major contributors to this measure. The decrease in self-stimulation at 10 months may indicate general inhibition of activity at this age. Since there is no reason to believe that the motor skills of children regress at 10 months in comparison to 6 months of age, an explanation that emphasizes regulation of stimulation through inhibition of motor activity seems plausible. It is also in keeping with evidence of increased latency to approach and grasp novel objects by this age (Schaffer, 1974) and with our finding of greater touching of the head and mouth and hand clasping, possibly serving the function of self-soothing.

Attack is a composite assessing a child's direct energetic responses to the stimuli presented. This variable was at its lowest level at 3 months and peaked at 13.5 months of age. Of its components, *bang toy* (hitting the toy stimulus with the hand or fist) was highest at 6.5 months. *Push toy away* (pushing, throwing, or attempting to push or throw the toy) peaked at 10 months and was maintained at 13.5 months. The 3-month-old infants did not show *pounding* (picking up a toy and banging it on the table), but it was seen at the older ages.

Regulation Via Approach and Avoidance. Approach is a composite assessing the child's decreasing distance from the stimulus. This variable was at its highest points at 6 and 13.5 months. Four specific behaviors made up the *approach* variable. *Reach* (the child fully extends the arm[s] to touch the object) and *inhibited reach* (the child does not complete a reach for the stimulus by complete arm extension and/or touching the object) peaked at 13.5 months. Infants at 13.5, 10, and 6.5 months also exhibited *lean forward* (leaning forward without extending the arms) more often than did 3-month-old infants.

Except for *pointing,* all other specific behaviors that were part of the *approach* composite showed a slight absolute decrease between 6.5 and 10 months, with a subsequent significant increase between 10 and 13.5 months. Increased motor skill contributes to the change between 3 and 6.5 months because reaching is not well developed at 3 months, but the dip at 10 months and increase at 13.5 months may be related in part to greater inhibition at this age (Schaffer, 1974).

Active avoidance is a composite assessing the child's increasing distance from the stimulus. It was not coded at 3 months, and, for the other ages, this variable was at its peak at 6.5 months. Of six specific behaviors constituting *active avoidance, arch back* (curving the back, neck, and head in a distinct arching pattern to the side or back against the chair) and *push back* (pushing the chair back and away from the table with hands, arms, or feet) did not show developmental changes. *Arm retraction* (pulling the arm or arms up and back, parallel with the head) decreased to its lowest point at 13.5 months. The remaining three variables—*leave chair* (child begins to get out of the chair), *lean away* (movement of the trunk away from the stimulus), and *withdraw hand* (drawing the hand back toward the body in response to the stimulus)—significantly increased between 6.5 and 10 months.

In *arm retraction* the child pulls the arm or arms back at least parallel with the head, resulting in a "hands-up" posture. Als, Lester, Tronick, and Brazelton (1982) observed this as either a one- or two-armed stress-related behavior in newborns and called it a "salute"; we observed only a two-armed version. This behavior decreases in frequency across age groups, whereas *withdraw hand,* where the child draws his or her hand back directly toward the body, increases over time. These two behaviors are similar in structure and function, but their respective developmental courses are opposite. Older infants demonstrate reaches more often than do younger infants, which may account in part for increases in the *withdraw hand* variable.

The slight decrease in overall avoidance across age groups may be related to the development of other late-developing strategies for regulation of environmental input. As an example, we can consider *push toy away* (pushing, throwing, or attempting to push or throw the toy). *Push toy away* increased between 6.5 and 10 months and peaked in absolute level at 13.5 months of age. This behavior occurred primarily in situations where a moving object approached the infant. In contrast to *active avoidance, push toy away* allows the child to maintain her or his position while at the same time increasing the distance between self and unwanted stimulus. By about 10 months of age children are not only capable of avoiding unwanted stimulation by increasing their distance from the stimulus through escape behaviors, but they can also achieve the same goal by pushing or striking the object away.

Regulation Via the Respiratory System. Heavy breathing (breathing accompanied by audible inhalations and exhalations) was at its peak at 3 months and decreased between 6.5 and 10 months of age. *Yawns* (inhaling deeply through the open mouth and exhaling) occurred rarely, and only at 3 and 6.5 months. *Sighs* (breathing in and letting out the breath in a forced exhalation) peaked at 6 and again at 13.5 months, the two ages of highest motor activity. Reductions in *yawns* may be related to the longer alert periods in older infants, and reductions in *heavy breathing* may be related to maturation of the respiratory system.

Lack of Sex Differences. Overall, only three of the variables investigated showed sex differences: *lean toward mother, arm movement 1,* and *arm movement 2.* For all three behaviors, females' scores were significantly higher than males'. One would expect that three of the forty-five tests of sex differences performed would be significant by chance. We thus concluded that no pattern of sex differences in these behaviors was evident in our data. Predicted sex differences in oral behaviors (from Korner, 1973) were not found, although differential subject attrition by gender may have contributed to the lack of differences observed.

Stability Analysis. Between 3 and 6.5 months and the later ages, few self-regulatory behaviors showed significant intra-individual stability. Between 10 and 13.5 months, however, *approach* ($r = .35$), *hand-mouth 2* ($r = .66$), *hand-mouth* ($r = .48$), *mouthing* ($r = .30$), *pointing* ($r = .34$), *repeated hand movement* ($r = .33$), *reach* ($r = .39$), *withdraw hand* ($r = .31$), and *overall disengagement of attention* ($r = .30$) all showed significant levels of stability.

The variables *hand-mouth* and *hand-mouth 2* showed stability in the medium range across two consecutive intervals, between 6.5, 10, and 13.5 months of age (r's for *hand-mouth 2* = .54, .58, and .66, respectively). With the exception of these oral behaviors, scales measuring regulatory variables did not show a great deal of stability from one age to another. However, the number of stable behaviors between 10 and 13.5 months suggests that some consistency of self-regulatory response over time may be developing.

Self-Regulation, Activity, and Emotionality. In relating self-regulation to other temperamental variables as assessed by the IBQ, we tested whether activity level is negatively related to hand-mouth activity and found the negative relationship expected on the basis of Escalona's (1968) early work ($r = -.31$, $p < .05$). Fear scores were also positively related to inhibited reach ($r = .34$, $p < .05$) and negatively related to *approach* and *attack* (r's $= -.36$ for both, $p < .05$). Distress to limitations was positively related to *attack* ($r = .31$, $p < .05$), as expected.

We also examined the relations between self-regulation and probability of laboratory smiling and laughter and distress. Here we found, as expected on the basis of our findings with older subjects, that laboratory distress was negatively related to the child's overall *disengagement of attention* ($r = -.30$). Distress also tended (at the $p < .10$ level) to be positively related ($r = .25$) to *orientation toward mother* (in particular, to *leave chair toward mother, r = .40, p < .05*). Smiling and laughter in the laboratory was positively related to the child's *disengagement of attention* ($r = .29$, $p < .05$) and *active avoidance* ($r = .29$, $p < .05$) and tended to be positively related to *body self-stimulation* ($r = .25$, $p < .10$).

These results suggest that patterns of self-regulation such as disengagement of attention may be related in meaningful ways to the expression of affect at thirteen months. Inhibition is related to parent-reported fear, and disengagement of attention is negatively related to distress and positively related to smiling and laughter in the laboratory. The inhibition finding could be seen simply as cross-validation of IBQ and laboratory measures, given our definition of fear as distress and latency to approach intense and novel stimuli. However, the disengagement of attention findings are especially interesting in light of the attention-emotion links reported earlier in this chapter (Capaldi and Rothbart, 1990; Derryberry and Rothbart, 1988). Laboratory work by MacLeod, Mathews, and Tata (1986) on adults also suggests that anxious adults have special difficulty shifting visual attention from a negative focus.

Infants who showed greater distress also made a greater number of attempts to leave the chair toward the mother. To the extent that distress serves as a communicative gesture, this orienting behavior may describe a developing strategy for self-regulation that requires the mediation of the mother. In predicting from distress at 3 months to the general categories of self-regulation at 13.5 months, we found significant correlations for *clasp hands* ($r = .42$, $p < .05$), *hand-mouth* with no sucking ($r = .54$, $p < .05$), and *touch ear-head* ($r = .48$, $p < .05$). These behaviors predicted from 3 months appear to share self-soothing by touch only, which would be a particularly quiet form of self-soothing. Thus, early susceptibility to distress may predict later self-soothing, but not its more active forms. This is an interesting finding, but its replication would be necessary given the exploratory nature of this analysis. Finally, distress at 3 months predicted a tendency toward *overall disengagement of attention* ($r = -.27, p < .10$), with earlier high distress predicting later lower disengagement.

General Discussion of Developmental Change. Taking a general view of the developmental changes in self-regulation observed in this study, we note that infants at 3 months already demonstrated ability to stimulate or soothe themselves but engaged in few approach behaviors and, in our attentional studies, fewer attentional controls on visual-spatial orienting than did 4-month-olds. In comparison to 3-month-old infants, 6.5-month-old infants were more active stimulus seekers. They demonstrated greater use of organized patterns of motor behavior such as reaching, which showed further increases to 13.5 months of age. In attentional regulation, 6.5-month-olds redirected their visual regard toward inanimate aspects of the environment to a greater degree than they did toward their mothers.

In comparison with their behavior at 6.5 months, 10-month-olds appeared generally inhibited, showing less active self-stimulating behavior and more self-soothing. In attentional regulation, 10-month-olds also showed a significant increase in orientation toward their mothers. Increases in inhibitory capacity, self-soothing, and social communication thus appear to be hallmarks of development of self-regulation at 10 months.

In comparison to 10-month-old infants, 13.5-month-old infants were more active at seeking stimulation, showed less self-soothing, more approach, fewer avoidance behaviors, and more self-stimulating behaviors. In their attentional regulation, they further increased their visual regard toward human beings as opposed to inanimate aspects of the environment. They also showed greater gestural communication in pointing and an increased ability to move objects away from themselves rather than move themselves away from the objects.

In general, we observed a change from more palliative methods of self-regulation (for example, clasping, mouthing) to more active coping, and a decrease over time in near receptor activity, as suggested by Kopp (1989). Overall, there were no changes in frequency of attentional disengagement from stimuli after 6.5 months, but older infants were more likely to redirect their attention toward their mothers. The findings in our laboratory on disengagement of visual attention reported above and in Johnson, Posner, and Rothbart (1991) suggest that the major changes in disengagement occur between 3 and 4 months of age.

It should be noted that our study leaves open the question of whether these behaviors actually function to reduce infants' arousal. More detailed observational work and experimental study are required to address this question. Nevertheless, our research indicates that 3 to 13.5 months is a period of rapid development in self-regulatory behaviors, with little individual stability in their use other than in oral self-soothing, and with disengagement of attention continuing to be related to lower susceptibility to distress.

References

Als, H., Lester, B. M., Tronick, E. Z., and Brazelton, J. B. "Manual for the Assessment of Preterm Infants' Behavior (APIB)." In H. E. Fitzgerald, B. M. Lester, and M. V. Yogman (eds.), *Theory and Research in Behavioral Pediatrics.* Vol. 1. New York: Plenum, 1982.

Baillargeon, R., Spelke, E. S., and Wasserman, S. "Object Permanence in Five-Month-Old Infants." *Cognition,* 1985, *20,* 191–208.

Capaldi, D., and Rothbart, M. K. "Development and Validation of an Adolescent Temperament Measure." Unpublished manuscript, University of Oregon, Eugene, 1990.

Clohessy, A. B., Posner, M. I., Rothbart, M. K., and Vecera, S. "The Development of Inhibition of Return in Early Infancy." *Journal of Cognitive Neuroscience,* 1991, *4,* 345–350.

Cohn, J. R., and Tronick, E. Z. "Mother-Infant Face-to-Face Interaction: The Sequence of Dyadic States at 3, 6, and 9 Months." *Developmental Psychology,* 1987, *23,* 68–77.

Derryberry, D., and Rothbart, M. K. "Arousal, Affect, and Attention as Components of Temperament." *Journal of Personality and Social Psychology,* 1988, *55,* 958–966.

Escalona, S. K. *The Roots of Individuality: Normal Patterns of Development in Infancy.* Hawthorne, N.Y.: Aldine, 1968.

Goldsmith, H. H., and Rothbart, M. K. "Contemporary Instruments for Assessing Early Temperament by Questionnaire and in the Laboratory." In A. Angleitner and J. Strelau (eds.), *Explorations in Temperament: Contemporary Conceptualizations, Measurement, and Methodological Issues.* New York: Plenum, 1991.

Haith, M. M., Hazan, C., and Goodman, G. S. "Expectation and Anticipation of Dynamic Visual Events by 3.5-Month-Old Babies." *Child Development,* 1988, *59,* 467–479.

Johnson, M. H. "Cortical Maturation and the Development of Visual Attention in Early Infancy." *Journal of Cognitive Neuroscience,* 1990, *2,* 81–95.

Johnson, M. H., Posner, M. I., and Rothbart, M. K. "Components of Visual Orienting in Early Infancy: Contingency Learning, Anticipatory Looking, and Disengaging." *Journal of Cognitive Neuroscience,* 1991, *4,* 335–344.

Kaye, K., and Fogel, A. "The Temporal Structure of Face-to-Face Communication Between Mothers and Infants." *Developmental Psychology,* 1980, *16,* 454–464.

Klinnert, M., Emde, R. N., Butterfield, P., and Campos, J. J. "Emotional Communication from Familiarized Adults Influences Infants' Behavior." Paper presented at the biennial meeting of the Society for Research in Child Development, Detroit, Michigan, April 1983.

Kopp, C. B. "Regulation of Distress and Negative Emotions: A Developmental View." *Developmental Psychology,* 1989, *25,* 343–354.

Korner, A. F. "Sex Differences in Newborns with Special Reference to Differences in the Organization of Oral Behavior." *Journal of Child Psychology and Psychiatry,* 1973, *14,* 19–29.

Leung, E., and Rheingold, H. "Development of Pointing as a Social Gesture." *Developmental Psychology,* 1981, *17,* 215–220.

MacLeod, C., Mathews, A., and Tata, P. "Attentional Bias in Emotional Disorders." *Journal of Abnormal Psychology,* 1986, *95,* 15–20.

Posner, M. I., and Peterson, S. E. "The Attention System of the Human Brain." *Annual Review of Neuroscience,* 1990, *13,* 25–42.

Posner, M. I., and Rothbart, M. K. "The Development of Attentional Mechanisms." In J. Flowers (ed.), *Nebraska Symposium on Motivation.* Lincoln: University of Nebraska Press, 1981.

Posner, M. I., and Rothbart, M. K. "Attentional Mechanisms and Conscious Experience." In D. Milner and M. Rugg (eds.), *The Neuropsychology of Consciousness*. London: Academic Press, 1991.

Rothbart, M. K. "Measurement of Temperament in Infancy." *Child Development*, 1981, *52*, 569–578.

Rothbart, M. K. "Temperament and the Development of Inhibited Approach." *Child Development*, 1988, *59*, 1241–1250.

Rothbart, M. K. "Temperament in Childhood: A Framework." In G. A. Kohnstamm, J. E. Bates, and M. K. Rothbart (eds.), *Temperament in Childhood*. Chichester, England: Wiley, 1989.

Rothbart, M. K., and Derryberry, D. "Development of Individual Differences in Temperament." In M. E. Lamb and A. L. Brown (eds.), *Advances in Developmental Psychology*. Vol. 1. Hillsdale, N.J.: Erlbaum, 1981.

Rothbart, M. K., and Hershey, K. "Development of a Parent-Report Measure for Childhood Temperament." Unpublished manuscript, Department of Psychology, University of Oregon, 1990.

Rothbart, M. K., and Posner, M. I. "Temperament and the Development of Self-Regulation." In H. Hartlage and C. F. Telzrow (eds.), *Neuropsychology of Individual Differences: A Developmental Perspective*. New York: Plenum, 1985.

Rothbart, M. K., Posner, M. I., and Boylan, A. "Regulatory Mechanisms in Infant Development." In J. Enns (ed.), *The Development of Attention: Research and Theory*. Amsterdam, The Netherlands: Elsevier, 1990.

Schaffer, H. R. "Cognitive Components of the Infant's Response to Strangeness." In M. Lewis and L. A. Rosenblum (eds.), *The Origins of Fear*. New York: Wiley, 1974.

Ziaie, H. "A Short-Term Longitudinal Study of Behavioral Self-Regulation in Infants Aged 3 Months to 13.5 Months." Unpublished doctoral dissertation, Department of Educational Psychology, University of Oregon, 1988.

MARY K. ROTHBART is professor of psychology at the University of Oregon in Eugene.

HASAN ZIAIE is associate professor of psychology at Virginia Union University in Richmond, Virginia.

CHERIE G. O'BOYLE is visiting assistant professor of psychology at Arizona State University.

Important relational changes in the family system during the second half of the first year of life are brought about when children begin to walk.

Socioemotional Transformations in the Family System Following Infant Crawling Onset

Joseph J. Campos, Rosanne Kermoian, Marcia R. Zumbahlen

The purpose of the study reported here was to examine whether the new experiences brought about by the onset of self-produced locomotion affect the emotional climate of the family. Our working assumption was that the onset of crawling generates changes in the relation between infants and their social and nonsocial environments, and that such changes serve as setting events for changes in the quality and intensity of the expression of affect by both the parent and the infant.

The most pervasive reason for expecting important changes in emotionality in both the parent and the newly mobile infant is ecological in character. As infants begin to move independently, they are more likely to engage in behavior unacceptable to the parents, such as manipulating dangerous or fragile objects. These encounters make the infant a likely

Preparation of this article was made possible by grants from the Research Board of the University of Illinois at Urbana-Champaign, the National Institute of Child Health and Human Development (HD-25066), the Oregon Medical Research Foundation, the John D. and Catherine T. MacArthur Foundation, and the MacArthur Network on Early Developmental Transitions. We thank Stephanie Hanko-Sommers for help in designing the interview and the coding system and Sarah Chamblin for assistance in the conduct of the interview.

Address requests for reprints to Joseph J. Campos, Institute of Human Development, 1203 Tolman Hall, University of California at Berkeley, Berkeley, California 94720. Copies of the interview schedule and additional materials related to the coding of the interview can be obtained from the same source.

recipient of parental anger. Moreover, locomotion can be a sign to the parents that the infant is an autonomous being and now must begin to be responsible for his or her own actions. The attributions of responsibility by parents create expectations for infants to comply to the parents' rules of conduct; violations of those rules may then lead to parental anger during this process of socialization.

A second reason for expecting new levels of emotionality with the onset of locomotion stems from the close link that exists between an individual's emotions and his or her personal goals (Campos, Campos, and Barrett, 1989; Frijda, 1986). Indeed, emotions have been called the outward indication of the fate of a person's goals (Lazarus, 1991). Positive affect in the newly locomoting infant should increase as a result of new levels of self-efficacy as goals are attained; negative affect should similarly increase as a result of the frustration experienced as the infant's newly attainable goals are thwarted. With the onset of locomotion, then, the infant is likely to undergo a burgeoning of both positive and negative affect because self-produced locomotion generates the possibility of new goals, of new means to obtain those goals, and of new opportunities for clashes between one's own goals and those of social agents in the environment.

A third reason for expecting major changes in the child's emotionality with the acquisition of crawling results from the infants' mirroring of the emotional signals of others in their environment. The infants' crawling increases the number of opportunities for parents to use verbal and facial signals to control their infants' undesired behaviors, and to encourage the child to engage with environmental events and objects. Such signals can be the source of the experience of affect if the child is in a bland emotional state, or they can augment ongoing experiences of affect in an already emoting individual. For example, as infants show excitement and glee at their many new accomplishments, the parents become similarly excited. The child can be expected to become even happier as the result of noting the parents' joy.

Fourth, crawling also reorganizes the child's attachment system given the new ability of the infant to control proximity to the primary caregiver. Indeed, the capacity to seek proximity brings about the transition to the use of the parent as a discriminated attachment figure (Bowlby, 1969; Ainsworth, Blehar, Waters, and Wall, 1978). Specifically, locomotion affects the use of the caregiver as both a secure base for exploration and a haven of safety. According to ethological attachment theory, the new use of the parent as a differentiated attachment figure may then increase the child's sensitivity to maternal departures. As a result, new and higher levels of separation distress may be evident. In sum, by reason of ecological, motivational, signaling, and instrumental behavioral factors, crawling onset may be crucial for understanding changes in the emotional life of the infant (Mahler, Pine, and Bergman, 1975).

Although changes in the child's socioemotional development are likely to follow the onset of self-produced locomotion, very few studies have systematically investigated the social and interactional changes that follow crawling onset. The few studies that have been done report changes consistent with the theoretical notions outlined above. For instance, Gustafson (1984) conducted a study linking goal orientation, locomotion, and changes in positive emotionality in eight-month-olds. In that study, she demonstrated that infants who were able to move about via a walker smiled and looked more often to their parents than when they were out of the walker and unable to move. Kermoian (1986) showed that crawling permits new types of coping, and she demonstrated that the longer infants had been locomoting, the more discriminating they were in selecting a stranger with whom to interact. In addition, researchers have reported changes in communication associated with the onset of crawling: Locomotion has been reported to precede increases in infant social referencing (Garland, 1982) and to forecast dramatic improvements in the ability of infants to follow another's point or gaze (Telzrow, 1990).

The scarcity of existing empirical studies suggests a need for a more thorough and comprehensive study of changes in the infant's social and emotional interactions following the onset of self-produced locomotion. As a first step in examining these changes, we conducted an interview study with the parents of eight-month-old infants, comparing infants with five weeks or more of crawling experience and infants with no locomotor experience. In addition, we interviewed parents of prelocomotor infants of the same age who had walker experience. This third group was studied in order to determine whether locomotor experience or the maturation of crawling abilities is related to reported changes in the family system.

Methods

This study focuses on parents' perceptions of the changes noted within their infants' physical and socioemotional development, parent-infant communication, parental expression of emotion toward the child, and parental expectations of the baby after infants acquire locomotion.

Subjects. Sixty-two parents of eight-month-old infants were interviewed and their responses were classified into one of three groups according to their infants' locomotor experience. The *prelocomotor* group consisted of parents whose infants were unable to move intentionally (N = 7 male, 8 female). The *locomotor* group consisted of parents whose infants had at least five weeks of experience with prone progression (N = 15 male, 16 female), with most infants able to move forward eight feet within thirty seconds. The *prelocomotor-walker* group consisted of parents whose infants were unable to move by prone progression but had been moving about using a walker at home for at least four weeks (N = 8 male, 8 female). Most infants in this group were able to obtain a desired object at least eight feet away within thirty seconds.

The infant's locomotor status as reported by the parent was confirmed at the midpoint of the interview. The assessment was embedded in an observation of the child's motor, free play, and social behaviors. The locomotor assessment consisted of the parent placing the infant on the floor, moving eight feet away, and luring the infant with a toy. If the parent reported that the infant used a walker at home, the procedure was repeated using a walker provided by the laboratory.

All interviews were conducted with the primary caretaker: sixty were conducted with the mother and two with the father. An additional nineteen parents were interviewed, but their data were not treated further because they did not meet the criteria for assignment to one of the three groups of the study.

Interview. The interview dealt with changes taking place in the prior few weeks in (1) parents' and infants' emotionality, (2) parents' and infants' styles of communication, (3) infants' interactions with the physical and social environments, (4) infants' physical development and motor milestones, and (5) demographic variables. (Infants in the three groups did not differ on any demographic variables assessed, such as infant age, day-care experience, birth order, maternal age, or maternal education.)

The interviewer first presented the parent with a general question about recent changes in the infant's behavior, his or her own behavior, and the child's physical development, after which the interviewer posed more specific probes. The questions were designed to be appropriate for both pre- and postlocomotor infants and included many items about matters unrelated to locomotion. To further minimize acquiescence biases, parents were not told that the study dealt with the consequences of locomotor experience.

Procedure. Parents came with their infants to a living-room-like setting for the interview. The interview began with a request for background information on the parents and the family. Once the parent felt comfortable, the interview was conducted in a standard order, except when a parent's response to one question covered information relevant to a later question. The entire interview was audiotaped with a small, unobtrusive recorder for later transcription.

At the midpoint of the hour-long session, the interviewer videotaped five minutes of free play, five minutes of parent-child interaction, and five minutes of the child's motor behavior.

Coding. The interviews were transcribed verbatim. Transcripts of approximately 25 percent of the interviews were examined, from which were created questions that could be scored by coders as a "yes" or a "no." The content of the yes-no questions reflected the theoretical issues described in the introduction of this chapter.

Two coders who were blind to the hypotheses of the study independently assigned yes-no responses (or "unscorable") to each of the questions while looking at the transcript of the interview. (A response was considered unscorable when the parent did not comment on the issue.) Intercoder reliability computed by Cohen's Kappa coefficient ranged from .71 to .97 (M = .83).

    Statistical Analyses. Data were analyzed using two-tailed chi-square statistics comparing the proportion of yes answers between all endogenously locomoting infants (that is, those able to crawl, regardless of whether they also had walker experience; N = 32) and prelocomotor infants (that is, those without any walker experience; N = 15). A second set of analyses compared the performance of the two endogenously precrawling groups (those with walker experience and those without).

Results

The major hypotheses of the study concerned changes in the family system following the acquisition of self-produced locomotion by the infant. Crawling was expected to influence the parents' attributions of responsibility to their infants and their communication of negative emotions. Although we had no specific hypotheses about changes in the parents' attachment behaviors toward their infants, we include here unexpected findings related to changes in the expression of affection by parents of locomotor infants. Table 2.1 presents the findings from this part of the interview.

Table 2.1. Changes in the Parent: Proportions of Subjects Rated as a "Yes" Across Locomotor Status

	Locomotor Status				
	Prelocomotors	Locomotors	χ^2	Prelocomotor-Walkers	χ^2
Increased expectations of compliance	3/13	20/29	7.6	8/15	9.1
Increased use of verbal prohibitions	9/15	31/31	14.3	13/16	n.s.
Increased use of voice for discipline	2/11	18/24	9.9	6/15	n.s.
Increased expressions of anger	7/14	28/31	9.1	13/16	n.s.
Use of physical punishment	0/15	12/31	7.0	6/16	7.0
New/intense forms of affection	3/14	15/27	n.s.	5/16	n.s.

Note: All statistical comparisons of prelocomotors with locomotors and of prelocomotors with prelocomotor-walkers were two-tailed (χ^2 = 5.42, p < .05).

Changes in the Family System: The Parent. Parents of locomotor infants reported a number of changes in their behaviors within the prior few weeks that were not as frequently reported by parents of prelocomotors.

Parents' Expectations of Their Infants. One of the most pervasive changes involved attribution of responsibility to their infants. Whereas 69 percent of parents of locomotor infants reported increased expectations of compliance by their children, only 23 percent of parents of prelocomotors did so. Parents of locomoting infants typically reported that they now expected their child to stop, listen, and obey when they said "no." Consistent with the notion that this shift in expectation is related to locomotor experience and not simply to general age changes, parents of prelocomotors-walkers reported significantly more often than did parents of prelocomotors (53 percent versus 23 percent) that they had greater expectations of compliance by their infants.

Concomitant with these changes in attribution of responsibility to their infants, parents of locomotors also reported major changes in the frequency and manner by which they attempted to communicate their expectations to their babies. Every parent of a locomotor infant reported using verbal prohibitions, compared to 60 percent of parents of prelocomotors. They also reported an increase in the use of their voice for disciplinary purposes significantly more often than did parents of prelocomotors (75 percent versus 18 percent).

Parents of prelocomotors-walkers showed a trend to use their voice for discipline more often than did parents of prelocomotors (40 percent versus 18 percent); however, there were no significant differences in use of verbal prohibitions by parents of prelocomotors-walkers relative to parents of prelocomotors. These findings on prelocomotors-walkers suggest that parents of such children are likely to create expectations for compliance and use their voices to scold the infants, but they do not appear to back up expectations for compliance verbally.

In sum, the interviews revealed that when infants acquire the capacity to move about voluntarily (whether on their own or through the use of a walker), parents begin to treat their infants in a more mature fashion, posing greater expectations for their children to comply to their commands and using a greater number of verbal sanctions to ensure compliance.

Parents' Anger Toward Their Infants. A striking change reported by parents of locomotors involved the use of anger to regulate their children's behavior. The expression of anger by the parent was both verbal and physical. Significantly more parents of locomotors (90 percent) reported expressing verbal anger when prohibiting their infants than did parents of prelocomotors (50 percent). In fact, some parents of locomotor infants volunteered that the onset of crawling marked the first time that they had expressed anger toward their infants. A similar trend was obtained for reports by parents of prelocomotor-walker infants.

On occasion, the parents' anger directed at their locomoting infants extended to physical punishment (typically, a light slap on the hands). Only parents of locomotors (39 percent) and of prelocomotors-walkers (38 percent) reported physically punishing their infants. Such punishment usually came about when the infant seemed to understand the prohibition but repeatedly ignored the parent's angry verbalizations. When describing incidents leading to physical punishment, parents of locomoting infants often made statements that typified their new levels of expectations of compliance by their child, and their feeling that punishment had to be used because of the seriousness of the child's infraction (such as grabbing an electric appliance or touching the door of a hot oven), or the failure of other means to control their children's undesired behavior. The following anecdote typifies what many parents reported about the context for punishment: "If my baby doesn't listen the first couple of times around, then I just have to deepen my voice, and louden it a little more. And if it still doesn't work, then I normally get up and tap him on the hand. Sometimes that will work, and he'll back off."

Parents' Positive Affect Toward Their Infants. In addition to reporting major changes in expression of anger and conflict, parents of locomotor infants tended to report changes in the intensity and quality of expression of positive affect. Specifically, 55 percent of parents of locomotor infants reported expressing new forms of affection (for example, tighter hugs, rougher play, and verbal affection), as compared to 21 percent of parents of prelocomotors ($p < .07$). There were no significant differences in reports of expressions of affection between parents of prelocomotor/walker infants and parents of prelocomotors.

In sum, parents reported major changes in their attributions of responsibility to their newly mobile infants, in their expressions of anger, in the likelihood of using physical punishment, and in the manner by which they expressed their affection to their locomoting infants. With the exception of expressions of new forms of affection and increased use of verbal prohibitions, parents of crawling infants and of prelocomotors-walkers reported changes similar to one another and different from those of parents of prelocomotors.

Changes in the Family System: The Infant. In addition to changes in the parents following crawling onset, we expected that there would be important changes in the infant's affectivity. Crawling was expected to influence the infant's emotionality, in particular, the incidence, intensity, and patterning of a number of emotions. We expected anger to increase as a result of the infant's new goal-directedness and opportunities for frustration and negative communications from others. We expected changes in attachment stemming from the infant's new ability to control proximity to the parent. In addition to changes in emotionality, we also expected increases in attention to distal events as these events became more salient in the child's life, and increases in interactive play as the child became more able to control interactions with others. The findings of this aspect of the interviews are presented in Table 2.2.

Expression of Anger. The clearest change reported by parents of loco-motor infants was in the children's expression of anger. Eighty-nine percent of parents of locomotor infants reported an increase in the expression of anger by their infants, compared to 43 percent of parents of prelocomotors. The increased anger of locomotor infants was evident in two ways: First, when infants were frustrated in an attempt to reach a goal, locomotor infants expressed anger more often than did prelocomotors. The latter seemed content to substitute another goal or activity in place of the one that they were unable to reach or partake.

Second, locomotor infants changed their manifestation of anger in intensity and manner of expression. Locomotor infants were more likely than prelocomotors to show extreme displays of anger. Mothers commonly described locomotor infants as screamers when a toy was removed and viewed this

Table 2.2. Changes in the Infant: Proportions of Subjects Rated as a "Yes" Across Locomotor Status

		Locomotor Status			
	Prelocomotors	Locomotors	χ^2	Prelocomotor-Walkers	χ^2
Increased expressions of anger	6/14	25/28	10.4	9/15	n.s.
Increased sensitivity to primary caregiver's departure	5/15	22/31	5.9	6/15	n.s.
Increased wariness of strangers	5/14	19/30	n.s.	7/16	n.s.
New/intense forms of affection to primary caregiver	5/14	22/30	5.8	11/15	n.s.
Increased attention to distal objects/people	4/14	26/29	16.7	9/12	5.6
Increased checking back in previously prohibited contexts	1/15	21/31	15.1	8/16	7.1
Increased wariness of drop-offs	4/15	19/30	n.s.	7/16	n.s.
Increased engagement in interactive play	1/15	17/30	10.4	5/15	n.s.

Note: All statistical comparisons of prelocomotors with locomotors and of prelocomotors with prelo-comotor-walkers were two-tailed (χ^2 = 5.42, p < .05).

behavior as the onset of temper tantrums. By contrast, mothers of preloco-motor infants reported that their infants expressed their anger in less intense ways, for shorter periods of time, and in a manner that could more readily be ended by distraction.

In sum, locomotor infants changed in terms of both the frequency of angry responses to events and the manner by which they expressed their discontent.

Attachment Behaviors. Locomotor infants also showed changes in attach-ment behaviors, as evident in their intensified reactions to the departure of the primary caregiver, new forms of displaying affection to the primary care-giver, and greater probability of negative reactions to unfamiliar persons.

Locomotor experience seemed to heighten infants' reactions to the parent's departure. The majority of parents of locomotors (71 percent) re-ported that their infants had recently become more aware of their depar-tures from the room than they had been previously, compared to only 33 percent of parents of prelocomotors. This increased sensitivity was mani-fested by the children's pre-cry faces and by mild fussing. (Note that although these responses to separation were shown by both prelocomotor and locomotor infants, they were elicited primarily in infants with locomo-tor experience.)

A typical response by one of the parents illustrates the changes in sensitivity to the parent's departure, and the parent's conjecture that loco-motion is related to such heightened sensitivity: "If I leave [the room], she gets upset unless she's busy and doesn't see it. But as soon as she notices, she starts hollering. I don't think it mattered the first four months. When she started doing more, sitting up, crawling, that's when she'd get upset when I would leave."

In addition to the heightened level of response to parental departure, locomotor infants' emotional responses to departures appeared to be spe-cific to the primary caregiver. These reactions were not the result of being left alone, or of being left in the company of a stranger; they were reported to occur even when the child was left with a familiar person. In sum, locomotor experience seems to facilitate the infant's monitoring of proxim-ity to the caregiver.

The changes in the expression of attachment by locomotor infants were also evident in changes in positive emotionality. Although 73 percent of locomotor infants showed new or more intense ways of expressing affection to their parents, only 36 percent of prelocomotors did so. These new or more intense means of showing affection included hugging, kissing, and patting of the parent by the child. Moreover, these changes in the baby's affection were remarkably similar to the changes that the parents reported in their own behavior, suggesting the possibility that mirroring of positive affect was taking place, either from the infant to the parent or the reverse.

In sum, the pattern of heightened reactions to separation, and the expression of more intense positive affect toward the parent are consistent with ethological attachment theory concerning the role of locomotion in the development of specific attachments.

Level of Attentiveness. The sensitivity by the infant to the caregiver's departure described in connection with changes in attachment behaviors may have been part of a general increase in sensitivity to distal events. Locomotor infants were more likely to attend to both social and nonsocial distal events than were prelocomotor infants (90 percent versus 29 percent). The following is an illustration of one baby's change in attentiveness as reported by the parent: "Now she looks to cats in the other room, or up high. She has been watching since the last few weeks. When she was younger and you'd take something away from her, she wouldn't watch it. . . . Now she [does]."

Additional evidence for the change in locomotor infants' attention to distal events comes from the increased, spontaneous checking back with the parent, seen in situations where the parent had previously prohibited the child or had tried to get the child to comply to a request. Specifically, 68 percent of locomotor infants and only 7 percent of prelocomotor infants were reported to manifest social attentiveness in such settings. In response to the question, "Does [your child] check back with you to see if what she's/he's doing is all right," one parent answered, "She'll do that once in a while, if she knows it's something she's not supposed to do. She'll look at me like, 'Am I going to get in trouble or what? Can I do it again?' "

The greater sensitivity of locomotor infants to distal events was also shown by parental reports suggesting that their infants were becoming more sensitive to drop-offs. There was a trend for parents of locomotor (63 percent) and prelocomotor (27 percent) infants to differ in their reports of increased wariness or attentiveness to heights.

In sum, crawling seems to expand the infant's visual world, making it easier for the child to take in events at a distance. The expansion of the visual world seems to include breadth, depth, and extent of visual attention.

Interactive Play. Significantly more parents of locomotor infants (57 percent) than of prelocomotor infants (7 percent) spontaneously described their infants' play as interactive, defined in terms of games like peek-a-boo or chase. The changes in interactive play reported for locomotor infants are significant for several reasons: The infants seemed to be initiating the games, the games involved more than one person, the infant's partner was often not the mother but rather the father, a sibling, or a pet, and the games had simple rules that involved turn taking. The games were also usually marked by high levels of positive affect by both the infant and the social partner. Because these games were either not possible or not engaged in frequently by prelocomotor infants, the glee associated with the high arousal produced by the games was much more prevalent among crawling infants.

Changes Observed in Prelocomotor-Walker Infants. Contrary to our expectations, most of the prelocomotor/walker infants behaved more similarly to prelocomotor infants than to locomotors: As reported by their parents, prelocomotor-walkers did not show more anger or new forms of affection to the parent, nor did they show more sensitivity to parental departures, wariness of strangers, sensitivity to drop-offs, or interactive play. There were two exceptions to this pattern: Compared to prelocomotors, prelocomotor-walkers showed significantly greater attention to distal objects and engaged in increased checking back with the parent in previously prohibited contexts. Prelocomotor-walkers also tended to display new or more intense forms of affection to the parent.

Discussion

Link Between Infant Locomotion and Parental Behavior: The Role of Parental Attribution. The new ecological demands subsequent to the onset of crawling produce a change in the affective climate of the family, as evidenced by the parents' increased use of vocal prohibitions, by their higher incidence of expressions of anger, and by their initial use of physical punishment. These changes in negative affect are balanced by a number of important modifications in the parents' expression of affection to their children. We believe that these changes may stem from parental attributions motivated by their infants' new levels of self-efficacy.

Parental Anger, Prohibition, and Punishment. In observing their children's increasing control over their own actions, parents are likely to attribute to the infants a new form of intentionality and, possibly for the first time, to have expectations of responsibility by their infants (Mahler, Pine, and Bergman, 1975; Spitz, 1975). Although all of the parents in our study clearly acknowledged that their infants had goals and intentions, only the parents whose infants were moving about voluntarily began to expect their infants to choose "appropriate" goals. Specifically, parents of locomotor infants began to make new demands of their infants, as if to teach them right from wrong, and began to train expectations of compliance by the baby to parental demands.

The parents principally accomplished these goals by using their voices to regulate the babies' behavior. This use of the voice becomes salient because the parent finds it tiresome continually to remove the baby from a prohibited object; in addition, the parent may not be able to move rapidly enough to remove the child from danger. The voice is effective across distances, and, unlike facial expressions, it does not require infant orientation toward the parent. Most of all, the voice is peremptory, and it can be graded in intensity and modulated in tonal pattern to produce the desired effect of encouraging or inhibiting the child's behavior.

Perhaps the most significant evidence of the parents' new attributions of responsibility to their children are the reports, made only by parents of crawling and prelocomotor-walker infants, that they resorted to physical punishment to control their children's prohibited behavior. As was mentioned above, the typical context for use of punishment was one in which the parent's utterance of "no," even in a stern tone of voice, was not enough to gain the infant's compliance. The parent's use of punishment seemed multidetermined. It represents the parent's new concerns about socializing the child to parental goals, the increased importance to the parent that the infant meet parental expectations, and the parent's emerging recognition that verbal signals alone, in the absence of physical action, may not effect compliance by the child. Locomotion thus affects the parent's preparation of the child for entry into a new world full of social demands, physical dangers, and opportunities.

Parental Expressions of Affection. Although we had predicted changes in the infant's attachment system following the onset of locomotion, we did not expect the reported increases in the intensity of the parent's expression of affection. As was the case with expressions of anger, we believe that parental attributions of responsibility may pace the changes in parental affection.

One attributional change following the onset of locomotion is that parents give new meaning to the child's proximity. Before the infant becomes mobile, parents control the distance from the infant; afterward, the child assumes some control. The infant's initiative in moving away from the parent in turn may lead to changes in parental affection: What the parent loses in time near the child is compensated by increases in the intensity of affection when the dyad is close.

Another attributional change that may account for the new forms of parental expression of affection is the parents' perception that their locomotor infant is more independent, more like a "real person," and more fun to interact with. As a result, the parents show more "grown-up" affection, such as a shift from baby talk to adult verbal expressions of caring.

A third attributional change following the onset of locomotion is that parents perceive their infants as less fragile, and therefore better able to tolerate rougher and more intense forms of physical interaction. Locomotion, then, by changing parental attributions, reorganizes the parent's attachment system.

Link Between Locomotion and Changes in Infant Behavior: The Role of Intentionality. When infants begin to move about voluntarily, at least three changes take place in goal orientation and intentionality: (1) There is a greater dissociation in space and time between the child's use of means and attainment of ends. (2) The child is capable of using alternative means to attain a goal. (3) The child is more likely to attain goals independently, but also to encounter frustrations to goal attainment. These changes in intentionality appear to have major consequences for the infant's expression of affect and for social interaction.

Affective Consequences of Dissociation of Space and Time. The greater distances that locomotor infants are capable of negotiating result in heightened interest in, and attentiveness to, distal objects and events, a finding originally reported by Gustafson (1984). This greater interest in distal objects and events is probably due to the child's developing ability to incorporate these objects and events into his or her own activities. In brief, formerly unattainable objects such as plants and electronic remote control devices become graspable and manipulable to the mobile infant, and formerly capricious social objects such as pets and siblings can enter into interactive games such as chase. The expansion of the infant's visual world with the onset of locomotion thus complements an expansion of their life space—of the things that matter to the child.

Furthermore, the greater distance between parent and infant affects how the infant uses the mother as a haven of safety (Bowlby, 1969). As locomotor infants move away from their mothers to explore the environment, they are more likely to monitor the mothers' whereabouts in the interests of reestablishing proximity if necessary. They also begin to monitor their mothers' changes in expressiveness, possibly to identify the mothers' emotional reactions to what they are doing and to confirm the mothers' prior communications about their behavior. Thus, if the mother leaves the room or is out of view, the locomotor infant is more likely to recognize her departure and to be upset at her absence.

The changes in goal orientation and intentionality in the locomotor infant produce changes in affect related to the infant's emerging sense of temporal order. Because the child must locomote to attain these new goals, the temporal relations between the initiation of means and attainment of ends are more salient for the locomotor infant than for the prelocomotor. This conclusion implies that the locomotor infant must become resistant to distractions that are encountered as he or she moves toward a goal. The resistance to distraction results in greater anger when the goal is not reached, and greater positive affect when the goal is attained. The changes in intentionality thus may result in a blossoming of affectivity, a prediction central to Mahler, Pine, and Bergman's (1975) theory of affective development.

Affective Consequences of Multiple Means of Goal Attainment. The onset of locomotion increases the number of opportunities for the infant to encounter obstacles and to use multiple means to overcome such obstacles. The locomotor infant's new ability to use alternative pathways to attain a goal provides a new sense of mastery, the positive affect that accompanies mastery, and the heightened sense of self-efficacy that may be the basis of pride. Although the interview schedule did not include questions specifically designed to assess these affective consequences, the locomotor infant's engagement, enthusiasm, and glee in games of chase, so frequently reported by parents of locomotors, support the notion that intense positive affect accompanies the increasing scope of events that involve multiple means to an end.

Affective Consequences of New Independence and Encounters with Frustration. There were aspects of the parents' comments about changes in positive affectivity in the infants that, while not the direct focus of the interview schedule used in this study, corroborate the reports of parents in other studies of the consequences of locomotor experience (Bertenthal and Campos, 1990). Those parents concluded that their infants were noticeably happier as a result of locomotion. They reported that their locomotor infants were less likely to be bored because of their new perspectives on the world, their ability to determine proximity to the parents, the new ease of obtaining toys, and the greater capacity to seek novel events in the environment. The parents attributed the sharp rise in the prevalence of their children's positive affect to the new independence made possible by locomotion.

Another comment frequently made to us by parents in our study concerns a shift from frustration to euphoria, to more modest levels of happiness as the child consolidates locomotor skills. With respect to the initial phases of infant acquisition of locomotion, many parents have reported that their children became fussy and upset at the lack of coordination of their movements. (Whether the lack of coordination is frustrating because the coordination is needed to attain a goal or because the coordination is a goal in itself is a matter of debate.) Once a skill is coordinated, there is a very brief period of intense euphoria as the baby repeatedly practices the skill. The euphoria is then replaced with a more subdued, but also more pervasive, positive mood that contrasts rather markedly with the fussiness that preceded locomotion onset.

Link Between Locomotion and Behavior in Prelocomotor-Walker Infants: The Role of Ecology. The data from parents of prelocomotor-walker infants yielded patterns of findings that were quite different from those of parents of locomotor infants but, with some exceptions, generally not different from those of parents of prelocomotor infants. We believe that this pattern of findings can be explained by ecological factors. In this study, parents whose infants used walkers generally limited their use to the kitchen and, in the process, may have affected the manner by which locomotion influences social and emotional interactions.

When the range of locomotion is limited, the development of self-guided and goal-corrected movement is constrained. In the kitchen, not only is there minimal space for mobility compared to all other rooms of the house potentially navigable by the crawling infant but also there are fewer barriers to goal attainment (such as coffee tables, beds, and lamps). Furthermore, when the child moves the walker in the kitchen, that movement may not be self-guided because kitchen floors are typically slick and permit the infant to glide from place to place without purposeful and efficient control of their movement.

When the parent uses a walker as a device to keep the baby busy and safe rather than as a facilitator of self-produced locomotion, the functional consequences of walker use can be very different from those of crawling. Mothers commonly reported that they used the walker in the kitchen, while they prepared meals, to keep the baby entertained by giving the infant food and kitchen utensils to play with on the walker tray. The infant's emotional states related to exploration may thus be constrained. Nonetheless, the parent's need to gain compliance and to use discipline increases because the walker permits the infant new activities not necessarily desired by the parent. In turn, the parent's prohibitions and expectations of compliance may prime the infant to check back with the parent.

The setting for reorganizations in the attachment system may also be different for infants who use walkers compared to infants who crawl. When the infant is in a walker in the kitchen, the probability of the parent leaving and returning may be much lower than it is in other rooms. In addition, the infant may not be permitted by the parent to leave the kitchen, or the infant may not be skillful enough to negotiate a narrow doorway and accomplish the transition to a carpeted floor. The meaning of separation when the parent leaves the infant or when the infant leaves the parent may thus be different for crawling infants compared to infants who are prelocomotor but have walker experience.

Initially, the motivation to study prelocomotor-walker infants was based on a desire to disentangle the role of experience from that of maturation of crawling skills; our expectation was that similarities between prelocomotor-walkers and crawling infants would support an experiential interpretation of any reported changes in the family system around the age of onset of crawling. But we found that in comparison to mothers of crawlers, the use of walkers by the mothers in this study created a very different ecology for the children, with potentially different implications for the children's socioemotional development. Only in circumstances in which the use of walkers produces ecological changes similar to those produced by crawling should there be similarities in socioemotional or other behavioral outcomes. Because our interpretation of the differences between crawlers and prelocomotor-walkers is speculative, a study using direct observation to test the hypotheses mentioned above regarding family ecology is called for.

Locomotion and Epigenesis. The findings of this study, in conjunction with other studies on the effects of self-produced locomotion, suggest new directions for the investigation of motor development and developmental transitions in general. Historically, motor development has been studied as an end in itself. However, the findings on crawling suggest that changes in a motor domain can have dramatic effects on social and emotional development, as well as on parent-child interaction. Motor development does not simply reflect the emergence of behavioral responses; it is an organizer of broad developmental changes.

The research on the relation between crawling and psychological development also points to new ways of understanding developmental transitions. Rather than simply describing the structure of developmental changes and linking these changes to ages or stages of development, the present line of research emphasizes a more process-oriented and functional approach to developmental transitions. It exemplifies how development in one domain lays the groundwork for widespread changes in other domains.

References

Ainsworth, M.D.S., Blehar, M. C., Waters, E., and Wall, S. *Patterns of Attachment: A Psychological Study of the Strange Situation.* Hillsdale, N.J.: Erlbaum, 1978.

Bertenthal, B., and Campos, J. J. "A Systems Approach to the Organizing Effects of Self-Produced Locomotion During Infancy." In C. Rovee-Collier and L. Lipsitt (eds.), *Advances in Infancy Research.* Hillsdale, N.J.: Erlbaum, 1990.

Bowlby, J. *Attachment and Loss.* Vol. 1: *Attachment.* New York: Basic Books, 1969.

Campos, J. J., Campos, R. G., and Barrett, K. C. "Emergent Themes in the Study of Emotional Development and Emotion Regulation." *Developmental Psychology,* 1989, *25,* 394–402.

Frijda, N. *The Emotions.* New York: Cambridge University Press, 1986.

Garland, J. "Social Referencing and Self-Produced Locomotion." Paper presented at the annual meeting of the International Conference on Infant Studies, Austin, Texas, April 1982.

Gustafson, G. E. "Effects of the Ability to Locomote on Infants' Social and Exploratory Behaviors: An Experimental Study." *Developmental Psychology,* 1984, *20,* 397–405.

Kermoian, R. "Changes in Infant Social Preference Associated with Locomotor Experience." Paper presented at the annual meeting of the International Conference on Infant Studies, Beverly Hills, California, April 1986.

Lazarus, R. S. *Emotion and Adaptation.* New York: Oxford University Press, 1991.

Mahler, M., Pine, F., and Bergman, A. *The Psychological Birth of the Human Infant.* New York: Basic Books, 1975.

Spitz, R. *The First Year of Life.* New York: International Universities Press, 1975.

Telzrow, R. "Delays and Spurts in Spatial Cognitive Development of the Locomotor Handicapped Infant." Paper presented at the annual meeting of the International Conference on Infant Studies, Montreal, Quebec, Canada, April 1990.

JOSEPH J. CAMPOS *is director of the Institute of Human Development, University of California, Berkeley.*

ROSANNE KERMOIAN *is assistant director at the Institute of Human Development, University of California, Berkeley.*

MARCIA R. ZUMBAHLEN *is a graduate student at the University of Illinois at Urbana-Champaign.*

The acquisition of language changes the ways that children react to parental demands.

Emotional Distress and Control in Young Children

Claire B. Kopp

What resources enable young children to manage the negative emotions that arise in the course of their everyday lives? Elsewhere, I have suggested roles for cognitive, social, motor, and language mechanisms and have described the overall management process as emotion regulation (Kopp, 1989). In emotion regulation, the child learns to modulate emotions, particularly those that are negative, according to situational demands. The term *modulation* covers a diversity of control strategies such as reduction of a strong negative state in order to achieve functional responsiveness to an ongoing event, maintenance of a reasonable balance among positive, neutral, and negative emotions during everyday activities, and inhibition of an outburst when requested to comply with demands that are not to one's liking.

Emotion regulation has relevance to the development of self-regulation

This chapter is a revision of a presentation made at Arizona State University, Tempe, Conference on Emotion, Self-Regulation, and Social Competence, February 8-9, 1991. Support for the research reported here was provided by a grant from the National Science Foundation (BNS87-10228). Appreciation is extended to Adam Matheny for sharing data from the Louisville Twin Study. Special thanks are given to Bonnie Klimes-Dougan for her creative thinking about resistant behaviors and negotiation, critiques of previous drafts of this chapter, and data collection and coding. Appreciation is also extended to Dafna Brook, Tracy Silber, and Anne McDonough for their coding of cries; to Laurie Morrison, Sandra Kaler, and Irma Roder for collecting the data on the children; and to numerous other undergraduates who also participated in coding. Finally, gratitude is extended to the parents and children who participated in this study.

and compliance in young children. In self-regulation, the child adopts and internalizes an aggregate of specific kinds of standards for behavior (for example, safety concerns, recognition of others' possessions) (Kopp, 1991). Compliance, a component of self-regulation, involves a positive response to a caregiver's request, or to long-term adherence to a discrete set of demands such as not running in a parking lot or not climbing on furniture (Kopp, 1991).

When emotion regulation and self-regulation are linked, the child adopts standards for behavior and does so in conjunction with a relatively agreeable affect (Kopp, 1989). In effect, the child realizes that cries, tantrums, and outbursts are counterproductive in the long term and do not eradicate parents' expectations and standards. When does this linkage come about, and how?

These two questions are relevant to our understanding of early socialization. We know that socialization to standards begins in earnest during the child's second year (for example, Kopp, 1982; Maccoby and Martin, 1983), and child compliance to caregiver requests increases from the toddler through the preschool years (Gralinski and Kopp, 1991; Kucynski and Kochanska, 1990; Maccoby and Martin, 1983; Vaughn, Kopp, and Krakow, 1984). However, during this age period, there are times of emotional upheaval, particularly the tantrums of the "terrible twos" (Gesell and Ilg, 1943) that often arise as a function of caregiver requests. Thus, it seems likely that an association of self-regulation and emotion modulation emerges sometime in the third year or later.

Unfortunately, no studies have focused on these combined topics. Indeed, there is little information about negative emotions (with the exception of tantrums) during the toddler and early preschool years. This chapter begins to redress these gaps. My colleagues and I have examined instances of cries and have analyzed data on children's compliance, language, and negotiation strategies in response to maternal requests. Our observations were made during the course of home and laboratory visits in two samples of young children, each of which was followed for a year and a half. Three major questions were posed: How much crying occurred in the home and laboratory across the age span of fifteen to forty-eight months? How much crying occurred in response to a specific maternal request involving toy cleanup? How did crying compare to other forms of resistant behaviors observed during the course of toy cleanup?

I expected to find overall declines in the total number of cry bouts but was uncertain if developmental trends would emerge relative to cleanup requests. I was also uncertain how the amount of crying would compare, relatively speaking, to other indications of child resistance to maternal requests. In terms of mediating processes, I expected to find a tie between reductions in crying and increases in language skill.

Relevant Literature

Cries of Toddlers and Preschoolers. The infant cry has been extensively studied in terms of characteristics and age trends (for example, Braungart and Stifter, 1991; Lester and Boukydis, 1985; Brazelton, 1962; Campos, 1989; Demos, 1986; Emde, Gaensbauer, and Harmon, 1976; Gustafson, Green, and Tomic, 1984; Wolff, 1969). In contrast, few developmental studies have focused on children slightly older than infants. The extant cry data base is mixed with studies converging on temperament issues (Bates, 1986; Goldsmith and others, 1987; Rothbart, 1989), extreme shyness (Kagan and others, 1988), temper tantrums (for example, Gesell and Amatruda, 1941), and causes of crying.

Despite a dearth of developmental studies, unpublished data provide intriguing hints about the course of crying during the toddler years. Adam Matheny (personal communication, April–May, 1991), for example, has observations of two hundred young children in the Louisville Twin Study. The children were each observed during a forty-six-minute standardized laboratory visit (coded in two-minute intervals) in which the mother was present or absent at specified times. Child behavior was coded with the Emotional Tone Scale (unhappy to happy) from the Infant Behavior Record of the Bayley Scales of Infant Development (Bayley, 1969). In this data set, there is clear evidence of mean increases in negative emotional tone from twelve to eighteen months, a move toward less negative tone at twenty-four months, and a dramatic shift to more overall positive tone at thirty months. In terms of children who actually cried during their visits, the numbers are 28, 16, and 12 percent at eighteen, twenty-four, and thirty months, respectively. Clinical support for the age trends in the Louisville data is in Gesell and Amatruda (1941, p. 205), who noted that excessive crying, resistance, and tantrums were "not abnormal for the period from 15 to 18 months."

Age trends in crying and possible causes were examined in a small pilot study done at the University of California, Los Angeles, with four males who were nineteen, twenty-two, twenty-six, and thirty months of age. All were observed in the Psychology Department's infant day-care program during a three-week period. Thirty-four crying episodes were documented in sixty hours of observation time. The nineteen-month-old had the most upsets, the two oldest children the least. Of importance, the twenty-six- and the thirty-month-olds demonstrated reasonably well developed language repertoires, whereas the youngest child had a very limited corpus of words. For all four children, cries were most common around caregiving episodes (for example, diaper change), subsequent to physical hurts such as falls, and upon separation from parents.

The relevance of language production skills to some forms of oppositional behavior and negative emotions was underscored by Reynolds (1928). In describing age trends in negative behavior, she remarked, " 'No!'

it must be remembered, is about the only tool which the two-year-old has at his command to express his unwillingness to do as we wish him to. The four-year-old uses 'Yes, I will in just a minute,' 'Wait 'til I get through doing this,' and other politer forms, just as adults do under similar circumstances" (p. 122). The point is that most children who are between eighteen and twenty-four months comprehend far more than they can talk about (see, for example, Bates, Bretherton, and Snyder, 1988; Lifter and Bloom, 1989), and intense frustration may result from the inability to communicate. Indeed, Victor Denenberg (personal communication, April 1990) drew an analogy between comprehending, nontalking young children and adult aphasics who understand but cannot speak.

Data collected decades ago are informative about other causes of crying. Jones (Jones and Burks, 1936) reported that interference in activities, fear, and frustration were frequent reasons for crying among a sample of sixteen-month- to three-year-old children who were temporarily in institutional care. In a similar vein, Blatz (1930) studied two- to five-year-olds in a nursery school and found child drop-off time at school as well as enforced conformity to school routines provoked the most crying among the younger-aged children. In contrast, hurts and interference with ongoing activities led to crying among the older children.

In sum, a small data base suggests developmental trends in crying among toddlers and preschoolers, with a possible peak midway in the second year. Age-related reasons for crying are also identified and range from caregiver demands and situational factors to limited use of language.

Noncompliance and Resistant Behaviors. Children are often unable or unwilling to go along with caregiver requests, particularly those that involve standards for behavior (for example, "stop playing," "it's time to go to bed," "don't walk with your glass of juice," "pick up your toys"). A number of terms have been used to characterize these nonresponsive acts, including resistance, negativism, contrariness, negative suggestibility, and noncompliance (Crockenberg and Litman, 1990; Jones and Burks, 1936; Kuczynski and Kochanska, 1990; Reynolds, 1928; Vaughn, Kopp, and Krakow, 1984; Wenar, 1982). Crying enters the picture because it can be the way that a child shows nonresponsivity to a caregiver request. Although tantrums are the most well known, children cry with considerably less intensity when showing displeasure with a demand.

Along with others (for example, Kuczynski, 1991), I have been concerned with the imprecision reflected in the most current, and commonly used term, *noncompliance*. The reason is straightforward: The toddler and young preschooler demonstrate a rich array of behaviors during a noncompliant act. This richness is lost when all behaviors are grouped together within a single category.

Thus, one of my recent goals has been to redefine our terminology and our coding schemes so that we can more fully explore nonresponsive behaviors. In conjunction with this goal, my research aim is to demonstrate how some discrete, noncompliant behaviors reflect differential levels of maturity, and how some quite effectively serve the child's autonomous needs. In my view, crying, for example, is one of the least mature forms of resistant behavior because it implies that the child has no other resources to call upon to handle onerous situations. In effect, crying terminates mutual discussion at any level of communication. In contrast, negotiations are a mature form of resistance. They are often resourceful in nature and speak to the child's ability to maintain the interaction with a caregiver despite displeasure with the caregiver's request. The negotiation may ultimately end with the child doing the caregiver's bidding, but the child has had an opportunity to introduce self needs along the way.

The following definitions reflect the current ideas of my colleagues and I about terminology. *Noncompliance* is the superordinate category of our typology and includes responses in which the child cannot or will not go along (in any way) to a caregiver's bid or request. Noncompliance may or may not be intentional and encompasses instances where children do not comply because they do not comprehend the request (Kaler and Kopp, 1990), forgot a previously stated prohibition, or did not process the event that occurred (see Figure 3.1).

Resistance is a major component of noncompliance and subsumes cases in which the toddler-preschooler appears to have some degree of understanding of the caregiver's request and does not comply. Components of resistance include *negativism* (refusals), which involves instances in which the child says "No!" or "I won't" or shows physical negation such as throwing or kicking; *cries*, which signal the child's displeasure with a request and imply a lack of alternatives for seeking a better solution; *ignore*, which applies to instances in which the child acts as if a request is not heard; *argue*, which covers situations in which "Why do I have to?" is a common query; and *off-task negotiation*, which subsumes attempts to modify a caregiver's request away from his or her original intent so that the end point is more acceptable to the child. Behaviors included in off-task negotiation are excuses, justifications, and bargains (see Figure 3.1).

Although contemporary investigators of compliance, noncompliance,

Figure 3.1. Typology of Noncompliant Behaviors in Young Children

Noncomprehension

Comprehension
  Resistant behaviors
    Cries/Tantrums
    Negativism (refusals)
    Ignore
    Argue
    Off-task negotiation

and resistance are attempting to broaden analytic frameworks and coding systems, there is an older literature that helps frame the nature of resistance in young children. The research studies in this genre primarily contained global definitions of resistant behaviors, but the findings are valuable for the general documentation of age trends.

Developmental studies of resistance and negativism abound from the 1920s and 1930s, perhaps due to interest in Freud as well as to the burgeoning nursery school movement. The findings from these studies, when viewed together, reveal agreement about age trends. In a substantive review, Reynolds (1928) reported a peak of resistantlike behavior at about two years, with a steady decline to age four years. Jones and Burks's (1936) summary, primarily covering studies published from the late 1920s into the 1930s, showed considerable agreement about a peak period of resistance at two and one-half to three years and also noted declines by age four. In addition, mediating variables were examined in a number of studies and included intelligence, gender, situational factors, and comprehension of commands. The findings are equivocal for a relation of negativism with both intelligence and gender.

An intriguing study by Weiss (1934) examined patterns of negativism among children, between thirty months and sixty-eight months of age, who received eight commands in three experimental situations. Negative behaviors demonstrated by younger children included repetitive acts, prolonged responses, and unrelated substitute activities, whereas the older children questioned, expressed dislike, and engaged in related substitute activities. The substitute activities may be akin to our current views of young children's negotiation, a point I return to later.

In summary, developmental trends have been reported since the late 1920s for a decline in resistant behaviors from the early toddler years into the preschool period. The decline is consonant with more recent reports that have focused on child compliance. Most investigators did not distinguish among the kinds of behaviors that were classified as resistant or negative, and crying was rarely discussed as a form of resistance.

A Longitudinal Study of Self-Regulation

Sixty-eight children and their mothers participated in our research in which the major aim was to systematically explore self-regulation in children. Two cohorts were formed: Thirty-one children (sixteen males and fifteen females) entered the study between the ages of thirteen and fifteen months, and thirty-seven children (sixteen males and twenty-one females) entered the study around thirty months of age. The two groups were followed for approximately eighteen months. Attrition in both samples was low (6 percent).

Children and mothers were recruited from local toddler and nursery school programs. All children were normally developing. The sample was primarily Caucasian and came from middle- to upper-middle-class families. Mothers in both groups were well educated. Maternal ages ranged from twenty-three to forty-eight years. Seventy-two percent of the younger children and 50 percent of the older children had no siblings when they entered the study.

The children and their mothers were seen in home and laboratory visits at set intervals: thirteen to fifteen, eighteen, twenty-one, twenty-four, and thirty months for the younger group, and thirty, thirty-six, forty-two, and forty-eight months for the older group. During the first visit, background demographic data were obtained. Each home visit was designed to be low key and to gain insight about mothers and children at home. Mothers of the younger children engaged the children in a teaching task and in a toy cleanup task, whereas mothers of the older children presented them with short vignettes dealing with situations where rules arise. There was also a toy cleanup that came at the end of a free-play period. Laboratory visits were more structured than home visits and included snack time, free play, and cleanup for the younger children. The older children had periods devoted to structured and unstructured play, delay tasks, and toy cleanup and were also given measures designed to elicit their knowledge of rules and reasons for rules. Home and laboratory visits were videotaped.

Observations and data collection were conducted by graduate and undergraduate students selected for their sensitivity to children and their mothers. All members of the research team were instructed to let mother and child maintain the kind of communication and rapport that was most comfortable to them. As noted below, child upsets occurred with regularity despite our good intentions.

Coding. Details about measures and coding schemes are reported elsewhere (for example, Klimes-Dougan and Kopp, 1991). Here, I refer only to codes for crying. All cries that were on the videotapes were coded, irrespective of the activity that was taking place or the location. Each upset was coded for activity (task or situation), duration, primary type (frets or cries, temper tantrum), precipitating factors if known, words that the child emitted during the upset, and resolution of the upset. Three duration categories were arbitrarily established: bouts that lasted two to twenty seconds, twenty-one to sixty seconds, and more than one minute. The category two to twenty seconds reflected the numerous brief cry episodes that were characteristic of the younger children.

Developmental Trends in Crying. A total of 101 incidents of crying occurred during home and laboratory visits (between fifteen and forty-eight months), with 88 of these from the children in the younger sample. The most cries were recorded between fifteen and twenty-four months, with a temporary decrease in cries observed at twenty-one months. This drop-off may be an artifact because there was no home visit at twenty-one months and the children were observed only briefly in the laboratory.

The total number of cries and mean scores, as well as the number of children who cried at each age, are depicted in Figure 3.2. As can be seen, by the time the thirty-month visits came around for the younger cohort, only one cry was noted. In contrast, at the thirty-month visits for the older cohort (their initial study participation), five cry episodes occurred, but cries were relatively infrequent after that point.

Figure 3.2 also reveals that the greatest number of children cried at twenty-one months of age and the least at thirty-six and forty-two months. The equivalent percentage of criers for each age is as follows: for the younger cohort, 20, 26, 30, 20, and 3 percent at fifteen, eighteen, twenty-one, twenty-four, and thirty months, respectively; and for the older cohort, 11, 5.6, 5.5, and 8.5 percent at thirty, thirty-six, forty-two, and forty-eight months, respectively. Tests of proportion revealed no significant differences among scores for the younger sample at fifteen to twenty-four months. Significant differences were found between eighteen and thirty months ($z = 2.07, p < .03$) and between twenty-one and thirty months ($z = 2.58, p < .01$). There were no significant differences among proportions of the older cohort.

With all age periods combined in each cohort, the data reveal that 50 percent of the children in the younger sample had one or more upsets, whereas only 20 percent of the older cohort ever cried ($z = 2.02, p < .04$). Six of the younger children cried at two separate ages (four of them at fifteen and eighteen months), and two cried at three separate ages. Two

Figure 3.2. Total and Mean Numbers of Cries by Age

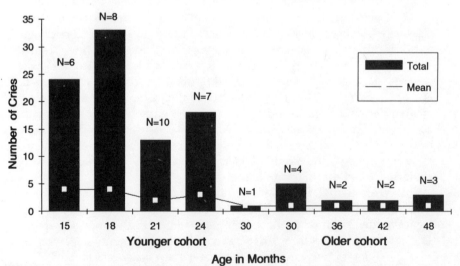

Note: N at the top of each bar is the number of children who cried in each age category. Mean numbers of cries are indicated by small open squares.

children in the older cohort cried on two separate ages. Gender differences in crying were evident at fifteen (five males, two females) and eighteen months (five males, three females) and generally equalized after these ages. Males were also more likely to be repeat criers than were females (six males out of a total of eight children).

The distributions of duration of cries showed that very brief cry bouts were relatively common during the fifteen-, eighteen-, and twenty-four-month visits and were not significantly different from each other. No brief cries were observed past twenty-four months. Cries at the older ages were generally divided between cries of twenty-one to sixty seconds and those lasting longer than a minute. In terms of cry type, temper tantrums were observed seven times, and three of those occurred at eighteen months. Table 3.1 shows the distribution of cries by age and length or type.

Was the distribution of cries a function of mother intervention? Frequency counts of the resolutions of upsets revealed that mothers intervened about half of the time irrespective of the age of the child. Among the younger children, there were many instances, particularly during the brief cry episodes, where the child distracted himself or herself and the crying ceased. These findings must be viewed cautiously because there were instances in which the investigator stopped videotaping when a child started to cry.

Finally, the incidence of crying was examined in terms of children who spoke only single words and those who had two-word sentences. This analysis was done for the eighteen-month visit because at this age there was considerable variability in language production. All but six of the children at eighteen months used single words, such as yeah, hot, plate, ball, truck, sit, high, doll, no, down, mommy, keys, oops, daddy, money, poop, and chair. In contrast, the two-word sentences of the six children

Table 3.1. Age Distribution of Short, Medium, and Long Cries

Age (in Months)	Type		
	Short	Medium	Long (N Tantrums)
Younger cohort			
15	18	3	3
18	27	3	4 (3)
21	3	4	6 (1)
24	11	6	1 (1)
30	—	—	1 (1)
Older cohort			
30	—	1	3 (1)
36	—	2	—
42	—	1	1
48	—	1	2

included "I do," "daddy swing," "my chair," "he's jumping," and "it down." Two of the six children also produced an occasional three-word sentence, for example, "bubbles all gone" and "I want ball." In addition, two of the six referred to themselves with "I," and one said "my."

The language production of the eight children who cried at eighteen months was examined. Seven of these children had single-word speech, and only one of these children combined two words.

In summary, these descriptive data reveal a pattern of crying that is largely confined to the period between fifteen and twenty-four months. Brief cries made up the largest proportion of cry episodes during these ages, and males cried more often than females at fifteen and eighteen months. Although there were only seven temper tantrums, three occurred at eighteen months. Inferentially at least, a limited language repertoire seems to relate to crying.

Crying Directly Linked to Toy Cleanup. In the previous section, all incidents of crying were grouped together irrespective of cause. In the following discussion, the focus is on crying that occurred solely as a function of a caregiver's request to put toys away. The request was made in each case after the child had been engaged in about ten to fifteen minutes of free play with a basketful of toys.

In addition to examining cries that arose in cleanup, two other kinds of resistance observed in the cleanup phases were also examined for the older sample only; these were refusals and off-task negotiations. Refusals included vocal responses such as "No!" and "I can't," whereas off-task negotiations included attempts to shift a mother's directive or request away from the cleanup, for example, "I am too tired," "I want to play with the truck," and "tell me a story."

Figure 3.3 shows the number of children who cried at each age, and the number who cried after they were asked to clean up the toys with which they had been playing. As can be seen, crying due to a cleanup request is proportionally lowest at eighteen months, and proportionally highest at twenty-one months for the younger cohort and at thirty and forty-eight months for the older cohort.

Whereas crying was infrequent among children in the older cohort, two other forms of resistant behaviors were common: refusals and off-task negotiations. However, both decreased across the age period from thirty to forty-eight months. For refusals, there was a main effect for mean score across ages (for thirty, thirty-six, forty-two, and forty-eight months, $M = 2.65$ [$sd = 2.94$], $M = 2.06$ [$sd = 1.89$], $M = 1.06$ [$sd = 1.53$], $M = .91$ [$sd = 1.36$], respectively) in a sex (2) by age (4), repeated measures analysis of variance ($F[2,28] = 7.48, p < .01$). Using a similar analysis, the mean scores for off-task negotiations ($M = 2.30$ [$sd = 2.34$], $M = 1.88$ [$sd = 1.89$], $M = 1.69$ [$sd = 1.51$], $M = .91$ [$sd = 1.02$], respectively) yielded a comparable main effect for age ($F[2,28] = 5.03, p < .01$).

Figure 3.3. Number of Children Who Cried in Response to Cleanup Request Versus Total Number of Children Who Cried, by Age

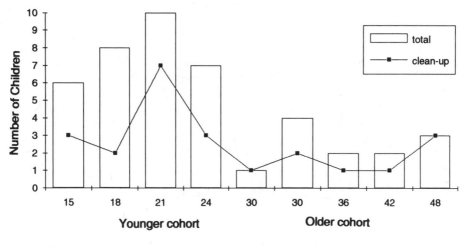

Figure 3.4 shows the percentages of children engaging in each of the three resistant behaviors coded in the cleanup: refusals, off-task negotiations, and cries. As can be seen, the percentage is lowest for cries and highest for off-task negotiations. Declines are obvious for refusals and off-task negotiations. What factor explains the developmental trend for off-task negotiations? Quite simply, by forty-eight months many more children complied shortly after the toy cleanup was requested by the mothers.

Inferentially, the ability to talk about self needs contributed to the decline of crying observed at thirty months and later. Increasingly facile use of language use likely contributed to the ability to negotiate, which at thirty months was a behavior displayed by most children. At this age, the children's language transcripts reveal a richness of questions, commands, and statements of self needs: "What is this for?" "I don't want to play." "I got buttons." "Press together!" "I can do it myself!" "Where's the top go?" "I want to say goodbye to him." "Put that over there!" "No gonna do it!" "Where's baby?" "I want these." "Mommy look!"

At forty-eight months, language narratives disclose knowledge of rules for behavior, humor, selfhood, play competitiveness, and bargaining: "There's no cleanup time here, never cleanup time here!" "Ok, mommy you want to hear another silly question?" "Mom I wanna look at this!" "I'm tired." "You forgot to . . ." "No, wait I can't get it!" "I want to see this now!" "Is it time to play with Play-Doh?" "I'm gonna win!" "Mommy, if I help can I have a doughnut?"

Finally, language, particularly at forty-eight months, was often intrinsic

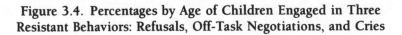

Figure 3.4. Percentages by Age of Children Engaged in Three
Resistant Behaviors: Refusals, Off-Task Negotiations, and Cries

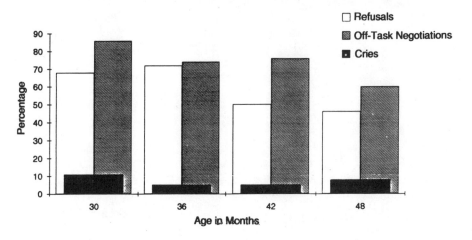

to episodes of crying: "Mommy, I don't want to!" The children would cry, sometimes with considerable feeling, but would talk all the while that tears streamed down their faces.

In summary, cries occurred as a function of the cleanup task with somewhat more consistency among the older cohort than among the younger. However, the proportion of cries among the older children was negligible when contrasted with their refusals and off-task negotiations. Moreover, these resistant behaviors declined across the age period of thirty to forty-eight months. Among the older children, language production was extensive, even during crying bouts.

Discussion

Three important findings emerge from this developmental analysis of crying and other resistant behaviors. First, between fifteen and twenty-four months, our data document a period of irritability and outbursts that appears to peak around eighteen to twenty-one months, among the 50 percent of children who cried. Although there were many brief cry episodes, the majority of temper tantrums also occurred during this age period (specifically, eighteen to twenty-four months). Second, the incidence of crying dropped markedly by the time the children were thirty months of age. Language may be a factor. Third, although crying was a relatively rare phenomenon in the third year (at least for the situations that we measured), resistant behavior was common. However, there was a linear trend revealing fewer instances of resistance between thirty and forty-eight months.

The irritability of some of the children midpoint in the second year supports Matheny's (personal communication, April–May 1991) data. Our findings revealed that eighteen and twenty-one months were peak periods of crying in terms of both the total amount of crying and the percentage of children who cried. Both sets of data suggest that the theme of the "terrible twos" needs some revision.

The eighteen- and twenty-one-month data were intriguing for different reasons. At eighteen months, crying was provoked by any number of events: having one's nose wiped, falling, wanting a glue stick (one of our props), having a jacket put on, and being asked to clean up. Denial of wishes brought on three tantrums. At twenty-one months, most crying was due to requests for cleanup. However, in addition to crying, there was also an unusual pattern of behavior that occurred occasionally. This was restlessness, observed particularly among four boys. These children did not play with as much interest as they did at earlier ages, and there appeared to be an increase in aimless wandering around the laboratory room.

The crying and restlessness present an intriguing developmental issue. Joanne Krakow (personal communication, 1991) has commented that restlessness, irritability, temper tantrums, and sleeplessness are fairly frequent among twenty-one-month-old children. In a similar vein, Megan Gunnar (personal communication, 1990) has informally observed children (about the same age) who seemed tense ("wired" was her term) and acted as if they were perpetually tired. Can these behaviors be associated with a more basic underlying phenomenon? Are explanations for these patterns of behavior tied to as yet unidentified physiological or biochemical changes that occur during the ages of eighteen and twenty-four months? There is, after all, other major behavioral growth that occurs between these ages. Might there be an analogue to the numerous physiological and behavioral transformations that occur prior to adolescence?

Alternatively, other factors are also worth exploring. It is possible that the data and observations reflect culture-specific influences that are found among American Caucasian toddlers reared in highly stimulating middle-class families. Toys, television, music, high language input, and fast-paced living styles often characterize the lives and surroundings of these families. Would similar trends be found among families whose live styles are very different?

With respect to the issue of language, this study at least suggests a role for language and crying, or lack thereof. Admittedly, many children at eighteen months had little language but did not cry. Thus, factors other than language were important in fostering or inhibiting the child's need to cry. However, my sense is that growth of functional and facile language skills reflects a developmental transformation that enables children to deal more effectively with frustrating situations. This functional role of language has been insufficiently considered as a factor in young children's outbursts.

Nonetheless, caution is warranted about my speculations because of the inferential nature of the data. Of equal importance, the children in this study came from families in which spoken language was highly regarded and where reasons and explanations were commonly provided to toddlers. A different pattern of findings might emerge in families that are less verbal, or even among children whose language skills remain somewhat limited past the toddler and early childhood years.

With respect to the pattern of resistant behaviors, the findings corroborate and amplify previous data on the developmental course of noncompliance behaviors. In our view, the demonstration of differential types of resistance is a distinct advantage. Crying, the least mature form of resistance, decreased rapidly, refusals showed a more gradual decline, and off-task negotiations showed a significant decrement but it was less than the decline found for refusals. The use of negotiation speaks to young children maintaining lines of communication. This strategy is probably less aversive to many parents than a simple no.

The data about off-task negotiations corroborate Weiss (1934), who reported the use of unrelated substitute activities as a form of resistance. Undeniably, the children in our sample who pleaded fatigue, who tried to get their mothers interested in another toy, or who talked about hunger were employing unrelated substitute activities.

In general, the developmental trends that emerged in this study support Wenar's (1982) view about transitions in resistant behaviors. Instead of examining children's physical forms of resistance versus their verbal behaviors, we focused in this research on a range of verbal behaviors (crying, refusals, negotiations). The data show that resistance does not disappear as language skills develop; rather, the child is able to introduce self needs in a more socially satisfactory and less emotional way.

Finally, comments are warranted about the cleanup task. First, in terms of task meaning, it is likely that requests to put toys away had little importance to the young toddlers. The children probably interpreted the requests solely as interruptions of pleasurable activities. In contrast, by the preschool years, children understand concepts of neatness and responsibility for cleaning up one's own mess. The task of cleaning up is intrinsic to most young children's everyday experiences. Thus, the older children in this study probably interpreted their mothers' requests very differently from the younger children, even though they demonstrated resistance. Second, performance on the cleanup task cannot be generalized to other situations where standards for behavior apply. Task demands, the salience of the situation, and demand familiarity have to be considered.

In conclusion, I suggest that the children in this sample largely demonstrated emotion regulation in an aversive situation (that is, the cleanup) by the time they were in the third year. This is impressive growth. Alternatively, the fact that half or more children at forty-eight months still showed one or another form of resistance when requested to put toys away indicates that self-regulation is still in the development process.

References

Bates, J. E. "The Measurement of Temperament." In R. Plomin and J. Dunn (eds.), *The Study of Temperament: Changes, Continuities, and Challenges.* Hillsdale, N.J.: Erlbaum, 1986.

Bates, G., Bretherton, I., and Snyder, L. *From First Words to Grammar: Individual Differences and Dissociable Mechanisms.* Cambridge, England: Cambridge University Press, 1988.

Bayley, N. *Manual for Bayley Scales of Infant Development.* New York: Psychological Corporation, 1969.

Blatz, W. E. "Emotional Episodes in Nursery Schoolchildren." In *Proceedings and Papers of the Ninth International Congress of Psychology.* Princeton, N.J.: Psychological Review, 1930.

Braungart, J. M., and Stifter, C. A. "Reactivity and Regulation Patterns in 5- and 12-Month-Old Infants: A Longitudinal, Multimethod Approach." Paper presented at the biennial meeting of the Society for Research in Child Development, Seattle, Washington, April 1991.

Brazelton, T. B. "Observations on the Neonate." *Journal of the American Academy of Child Psychiatry,* 1962, *1,* 38–58.

Campos, R. G. "Soothing Pain-Elicited Distress in Infants with Swaddling and Pacifiers." *Child Development,* 1989, *60,* 781–792.

Crockenberg, S., and Litman, C. "Autonomy as Competence in 2-Year-Olds: Compliance and Self-Assertion." *Developmental Psychology,* 1990, *26,* 961–971.

Demos, V. "Crying in Early Infancy: An Illustration of the Motivational Function of Affect." In T. B. Brazelton and M. W. Yogman (eds.), *Affective Development in Infancy.* Norwood, N.J.: Ablex, 1986.

Emde, R. N., Gaensbauer, T. J., and Harmon, R. J. *Emotional Expression in Infancy.* New York: International Universities Press, 1976.

Gesell, A., and Amatruda, C. A. *Developmental Diagnosis: Normal and Abnormal Child Development.* New York: Hoeber, 1941.

Gesell, A., and Ilg, F. L. *Infant and Child in the Culture of Today: The Guidance of Development in Home and Nursery School.* New York: HarperCollins, 1943.

Goldsmith, H. H., Buss, A. H., Plomin, R., Rothbart, M. K., Thomas, A., Chess, S., Hinde, R. A., and McCall, R. B. "What Is Temperament? Four Approaches." *Child Development,* 1987, *58,* 505–529.

Gralinski, J. H., and Kopp, C. B. "Everyday Rules for Behavior: Mothers' Requests to Young Children." Unpublished manuscript, Department of Psychology, University of California, Los Angeles, 1991.

Gustafson, G. E., Green, J. A., and Tomic, T. "Acoustic Correlates of Individuality in the Cries of Human Infants." *Developmental Psychology,* 1984, *17,* 311–324.

Jones, M. C., and Burks, B. S. *Personality Development in Childhood.* Monographs of the Society for Research in Child Development, vol. 1, no. 4. Washington, D.C.: Society for Research in Child Development National Research Council, 1936.

Kagan, J., Reznick, J. S., Snidman, N., Gibbons, J., and Johnson, M. O. "Childhood Derivatives of Inhibitions and Lack of Inhibition to the Unfamiliar." *Child Development,* 1988, *59,* 1580–1589.

Kaler, S. R., and Kopp, C. B. "Compliance and Comprehension in Very Young Toddlers." *Child Development,* 1990, *61,* 1997–2003.

Klimes-Dougan, B., and Kopp, C. B. "Developmental Trends in Resistant Behaviors of Young Children." Unpublished manuscript, Department of Psychology, University of California, Los Angeles, 1991.

Kopp, C. B. "The Antecedents of Self-Regulation: A Developmental Perspective." *Developmental*

Psychology, 1982, *18*, 199–214.

Kopp, C. B. "Regulation of Distress and Negative Emotions: A Developmental View." *Developmental Psychology*, 1989, *25*, 343–354.

Kopp, C. B. "New Ideas About Compliance and Non-Compliance Among Very Young Children." Unpublished manuscript, Department of Psychology, University of California, Los Angeles, 1991.

Kuczynski, L. "Emerging Conceptions of Children's Responses to Parental Control." Paper presented at the biennial meeting of the Society for Research in Child Development, Seattle, Washington, April 1991.

Kuczynski, L., and Kochanska, G. "Development of Children's Noncompliance Strategies from Toddlerhood to Age 5." *Developmental Psychology*, 1990, *26*, 398–408.

Lester, B. M., and Boukydis, C. F. *Infant Crying: Theoretical and Research Perspectives.* New York: Plenum, 1985.

Lifter, K., and Bloom, L. "Object Knowledge and the Emergence of Language." *Infant Behavior and Development*, 1989, *12*, 395–423.

Maccoby, E. E., and Martin, J. A. "Socialization in the Context of the Family: Parent-Child Interaction." In E. M. Hetherington (ed.), *Handbook of Child Psychology.* Vol. 4: *Socialization, Personality, and Social Development.* (4th ed.) New York: Wiley, 1983.

Reynolds, M. M. *Negativism of Pre-School Children.* New York: AMS Press, 1928.

Rothbart, M. K. "Temperament and Development." In G. A. Kohnstamm, J. E. Bates, and M. K. Rothbart (eds.), *Temperament in Childhood: A Framework.* New York: Wiley, 1989.

Vaughn, B. E., Kopp, C. B., and Krakow, J. B. "The Emergence and Consolidation of Self-Control from 18 to 30 Months of Age: Normative Trends and Individual Differences." *Child Development*, 1984, *55*, 990–1004.

Weiss, L. A. "An Experimental Investigation of Certain Factors Involved in the Preschool Child's Compliance with Commands." *University of Iowa Studies in Child Welfare*, 1934, *9* (3), 129–157.

Wenar, C. "On Negativism." *Human Development*, 1982, *25*, 1–23.

Wolff, P. H. "The Natural History of Crying and Other Vocalizations in Early Infancy." In B. M. Foss (ed.), *Determinants of Infant Behavior.* Vol. 4. London: Methuen, 1969.

CLAIRE B. KOPP is adjunct professor of psychology at the University of California, Los Angeles.

Parents influence the ways in which children cope with their own and others' emotions, and this influence affects children's social behaviors.

Emotional Responsivity to Others: Behavioral Correlates and Socialization Antecedents

Nancy Eisenberg, Richard A. Fabes,
Gustavo Carlo, Mariss Karbon

Social interactions among children frequently involve emotion. Children laugh and smile during play as well as express anger, distress, or sadness (Fabes, Eisenberg, McCormick, and Wilson, 1988). Individual differences in the emotions expressed, in their modes of expression, and in the behaviors that accompany emotional reactions undoubtedly influence the quality of children's ongoing social interactions. Moreover, the ways in which children manage and express their emotions are likely to be correlates of children's social competence and popularity (Cummings and Cummings, 1988; Denham, 1986; Fabes and Eisenberg, in press).

Thus, it is surprising that there is relatively little research concerning the roles of children's emotional reactions and self-regulation in their social behavior with peers. In regard to negative affect, researchers have found that feelings of sadness are associated with helping, sharing, or comforting others, particularly if the negative emotion is an empathic reaction to another's negative state or condition (Carlson and Miller, 1987; Eisenberg and Fabes, 1991). However, at least among younger children, expressions

This research was supported by a grant from the National Science Foundation (BNS88-07784) to the first two authors, and Career Development and Research Scientist Development Awards from the National Institute of Child Health and Development (K04 HD00717) and the National Institute of Mental Health (K02 MH00903-01) to Nancy Eisenberg.

of anger do not elicit positive behaviors from peers; rather, children tend to leave those who express anger (Denham, 1986). Indeed, anger frequently seems to be the cause of aggression (for example, Camras, 1977; Cummings and Cummings, 1988), and hostile aggression seems to be associated with peer rejection (Coie, Dodge, and Kupersmidt, 1990) and with indexes of maladjustment (for example, criminal activity) in adolescence and adulthood (Parker and Asher, 1987).

In social interactions, children experience negative emotion based not only on their own direct experience but also on vicariously induced negative emotional reactions. Moreover, there are individual differences in how children deal with vicariously induced emotional arousal. Vicariously induced anger can result in disregulated behavior, behavioral constriction, or concern for the person or persons expressing the anger, depending on the child's style of coping with the emotion (Cummings and Cummings, 1988). In addition, as noted previously, children exposed to others' sadness, distress, or need sometimes experience empathy (that is, experience the same, or nearly the same, emotion as the other person), sympathy (that is, other-oriented concern and sorrow based on the apprehension of the other's emotion or condition), or personal distress (that is, a self-focused, aversive reaction such as anxiety or discomfort in response to apprehension of another's emotional state or condition). Children who experience sympathy frequently try to assist others in distress (Eisenberg and Fabes, 1991); in contrast, children who are anxious or distressed in reaction to others' negative emotions often avoid dealing with the distressing situation or may even respond aggressively (Eisenberg and Fabes, 1991; Eisenberg, Fabes, Miller, and others, 1990; Radke-Yarrow and Zahn-Waxler, 1984).

The aforementioned research on aggression, anger, and empathy suggests that some children are able to deal with their emotions in a constructive manner in social contexts, whereas other children have difficulty regulating their emotional reactions and emotion-related behaviors. An important question concerns the person variables that are associated with constructive versus less constructive and more disregulated emotional and behavioral reactions, and the origins of these differences. In the present chapter, we address these issues in two ways. First, we discuss research findings concerning individual differences in children that appear to be associated with their vicarious emotional responding and their tendency to engage in prosocial behaviors. As part of this discussion, we propose possible dispositional and stylistic characteristics that may contribute to the pattern of individual differences that we have observed. Then we focus on research concerning the socialization of emotions, for example, sympathy and anger expressed during peer interactions.

Individual Differences

Looking across a series of studies on preschoolers' and elementary school children's vicariously induced emotional reactions and prosocial behavior (voluntary behavior intended to benefit another), at least two clusters of behaviors seem to emerge. Some children appear to be particularly likely to spontaneously help or share, without being asked to do so. These children are relatively social and assertive (Eisenberg, Cameron, Tryon, and Dodez, 1981; Eisenberg, Pasternack, Cameron, and Tryon, 1984), sympathetic (Eisenberg, McCreath, and Ahn, 1988), and emotionally expressive (although the valence of their expressiveness is not always positive) in response to peers' positive behaviors (Eisenberg, Cameron, Tryon, and Dodez, 1981). In addition, high frequency of spontaneous prosocial behaviors has been associated with relatively low levels of egoistic moral reasoning and relatively high levels of other-oriented, primitive empathic reasoning (that is, needs-oriented prosocial moral reasoning; Eisenberg, Pasternack, Cameron, and Tryon, 1984; Eisenberg-Berg and Hand, 1979).

In contrast, children who exhibit high levels of compliant prosocial behavior—sharing or helping behavior in response to a peer's verbal or nonverbal request—appear to be relatively nonassertive (Eisenberg, Cameron, Tryon, and Dodez, 1981; Eisenberg, Pasternack, Cameron, and Tryon, 1984; Eisenberg, Fabes, Miller, and others, 1990; Larrieu, 1984) and prone to experience personal distress (which, in general, is associated with low levels of altruistic behavior; Eisenberg and Fabes, 1991) when directly confronted with another person in distress or need (Eisenberg, Fabes, Miller, and others, 1990; Eisenberg, McCreath, and Ahn, 1988). In addition, particularly for boys, these children seem to be considered easy targets by their peers. That is, they are frequently asked by peers for help or for a possession and they tend to receive negative rather than positive reactions from peers when they assist (Eisenberg, Cameron, Tryon, and Dodez, 1981; Eisenberg, McCreath, and Ahn, 1988). Moreover, children who frequently perform compliant prosocial behaviors are less sociable than are children who are high in spontaneous prosocial behavior, although they are not extremely low in social interactions (Eisenberg, Cameron, Tryon, and Dodez, 1981). Unlike spontaneous prosocial behavior, compliant prosocial behavior does not seem to be related to children's prosocial moral reasoning (Eisenberg, Pasternack, Cameron, and Tryon, 1984).

Although these findings are scattered throughout a number of studies, the pattern of findings is suggestive. Children who engage in relatively high levels of spontaneous prosocial behavior and are relatively sociable, emotionally responsive, and socially assertive seem prone to experience sympathetic reactions to others in distress or need and verbalize relatively mature moral reasoning when talking about prosocial dilemmas. Such chil-

dren appear to be well regulated in regard to both their emotional responding and their behavioral reactions in social interactions. In contrast, children who engage in high levels of compliant prosocial behavior, particularly
boys, seem prone to experience personal distress in some contexts and are
less socially adept than are children high in spontaneous prosocial behavior. In addition, both young boys and girls high in compliant prosocial
behavior are relatively nonassertive. These findings suggest that boys who
engage in high levels of compliant prosocial behavior have difficulty dealing
with their own and others' emotions and are not especially popular with
their peers. Although girls who are prone to personal distress also appear
to be relatively nonassertive, they are not particularly high in compliant
prosocial behavior (Eisenberg, Fabes, Miller, and others, 1990); indeed,
girls who react to others' distress with sympathy sometimes may exhibit
high levels of compliant prosocial behavior when engaged in dyadic play
(Eisenberg, McCreath, and Ahn, 1988).

In general, this pattern of findings is consistent with the argument that
individual differences in the regulation of emotion and in socially competent
behavior are intimately linked. Psychologists have suggested that overarousal
due to empathy results in self-focus (Hoffman, 1982) or personal distress
(Eisenberg, Bernzweig, and Fabes, 1992), and negative emotional arousal in
general also may be expected to engender a focus on the self (for example,
Wood, Saltzberg, and Goldsamt, 1990; Wood and others, 1990). If this conjecture is valid, individuals who are unable to maintain their emotional reactions within a tolerable range (and therefore tend to become overaroused)
can be expected to focus on their own needs and to behave in ways that may
not facilitate positive social interactions in situations in which negative emotion is salient. In addition, children who typically exhibit high levels of personal distress and other sorts of overarousal may have difficulty coping with
others' negative emotions or with asserting themselves appropriately in social
situations involving potential conflict.

Determinants of Level of Emotional Arousal

In our view, whether or not individuals become overaroused in social
contexts is likely to be a function of at least two person variables: (1)
individuals' dispositional levels of reactivity, particularly threshold and intensity of responses (aspects of temperament; Rothbart and Derryberry, 1981)
and (2) individuals' abilities to regulate (modulate) their emotional reactions
and cope with the evocative situation (Derryberry and Rothbart, 1988;
Lazarus and Folkman, 1984).

There is evidence that individual differences in emotional intensity or
reactivity are associated with emotional reactions in specific distressing or
stressful situations. For example, Eisenberg, Fabes, Schaller, Miller, and
others (1991), found that adults' scores on a scale of dispositional affective

intensity were positively associated with arousal (that is, skin conductance) in response to a sympathy-evoking film and reported distress to a distressing film. In another study with adults, Derryberry and Rothbart (1988) obtained positive correlations between measures of dispositional arousal and sadness. In addition, there is evidence suggesting that people who tend to react empathically or sympathetically to others in distress are relatively high in emotional intensity and low in the tendency to screen stimulation (Larsen, Diener, and Cropanzano, 1987; Mehrabian, 1980).

The second individual difference, relevant coping processes, can be viewed in at least two different but interrelated ways. First, coping as viewed by persons studying temperament involves self-regulation of impinging stimuli and internal states, using mechanisms such as attentional shifts away from an arousing or unpleasant stimulus to modulate distress (Rothbart and Derryberry, 1981). People who can regulate their emotional reactivity through allocation of attention can be expected to react more positively to stressful events (Fox, 1989). For example, the abilities to shift and focus attention have been negatively associated with reported susceptibility to negative emotion, particularly frustration and fear (Derryberry and Rothbart, 1988). In addition, infants high in intensity and distractibility, as well as low in threshold and adaptiveness, seem prone to develop behavioral problems, including aggression (Thomas, Chess, and Birch, 1968).

Second, coping can be viewed as changing cognitive and behavioral efforts to manage specific external or internal demands that are appraised as taxing or exceeding the resources of the individual (Lazarus and Folkman, 1984). Two general modes of this type of coping have been differentiated: problem focused (efforts to modify the source of the problem) and emotion focused (efforts to reduce emotional distress). Thus, coping behaviors include ways of modulating the degree of emotional arousal in a given situation as well as mechanisms for dealing with the resultant degree of emotional arousal and other factors (such as the behavior of another person) that contribute to overtaxing of the individual's resources. Although self-regulation and coping skills tend to be operationalized differently, self-regulation is an inherent aspect of some modes of coping (that is, some types of emotion-focused coping). Moreover, individuals who can regulate their emotional arousal are likely to cope in relatively constructive and controlled ways; indeed, Lazarus and Folkman (1984) argued that in most situations people first need to regulate emotional distress in order to facilitate problem-focused coping.

In our view, as in the views of others (for example, Fox, 1989), emotional arousability and self-regulation/coping skills interact in their effects on social behavior. For example, high emotional arousability, combined with high self-regulation and coping skills, is seen to result in positive outcomes such as sociability, social competence, sympathy, expressiveness, and popularity. Due to limited space, we do not elaborate on this issue here; the important point is that dispositional differences in emotional arousability and in styles of regulating emotion are relevant to an understanding of emotional overarousal and the development of socially competent behavior.

Individual differences in emotional arousability may be determined, in part, by biological factors given the clear evidence of individual differences in temperament from infancy (for example, Rothbart and Derryberry, 1981). However, the environment, including socialization influences, undoubtedly affects children's self-regulation skills, as well as the ways in which children deal with emotion-eliciting events in their environments (Gottman and Katz, 1989; Kopp, 1989).

Socialization of Children's Emotional Responsivity to Others and Methods of Dealing with Emotion in Social Contexts

There are a number of ways in which socialization agents may influence how children respond to and cope with emotionally evocative situations. First, socialization may affect whether or not children tend to focus on others' needs or on their own in situations involving vicarious emotion. The verbal messages that parents provide may help children to focus on others' emotional states and needs. For example, parental use of inductions (reasoning) that help children to understand the consequences of their own behavior for others appears to promote positive behavior, presumably because inductions promote empathic responsiveness to others (Hoffman, 1975). In addition, adults who are empathic in their parenting behavior may model an other-orientation to their children. This idea is consistent with the finding that empathic children tend to have warm, nurturant parents (who probably model empathy; Barnett, 1987).

Second, how socializers react to the expression of emotion in general, and if they themselves readily exhibit emotions, seem to affect the likelihood of offspring who decode emotions (Halberstadt, 1986) and report and exhibit negative emotions (Eisenberg, Schaller, Fabes, and others, 1988; Eisenberg and Fabes, 1991). Buck (1984) has suggested that sanctions for emotional expressiveness in the home are associated with physiological but not external makers of emotional responding in adults. This association is because children who receive negative reactions to displays of emotion would be expected to gradually learn to hide their emotions but as adults would feel anxious when in emotionally evocative situations (due to prior associations between punishment and emotional expressivity).

In addition, socializers may teach or model for their children ways of dealing with emotions. Whereas some parents may teach their children to hide or control their emotions, others may emphasize techniques such as seeking social support or dealing instrumentally with problems and stressors (Roberts and Strayer, 1987).

Third, socializers' willingness to discuss emotions with their children seems to relate to children's awareness of others' emotional states (Dunn, Bretherton, and Munn, 1987). Emotion-related language in the culture and in the family sharpens the child's awareness of emotional states, plays a role in the development of idiosyncratic or familial associations between state and phenomenology as a function of training (Lewis and Michalson, 1983), and promotes the development of schematic emotional memory and an abstract emotion-related conceptual system (Malatesta and Haviland, 1985). This latter development is important because emotional schemata seem to play a crucial role in the structuring of emotional experience, the blending of experiences, and the development of subtler feelings that are part of sympathy (Malatesta and Haviland, 1985).

Socialization and Vicarious Emotional Responding. In a series of studies, we have started to examine the role of socialization influences in children's and adults' sympathy and personal distress, and in their coping with emotion in social contexts. The results of several of these studies are consistent with the propositions outlined above regarding the socialization of emotion. First, in two studies we have obtained data indicating that empathic parents tend to have same-sex children who are sympathetic and/or unlikely to experience personal distress when exposed to others in need (Eisenberg, Fabes, Schaller, Carlo, and Miller, 1991; Fabes, Eisenberg, and Miller, 1990). Specifically, sympathetic mothers tend to have daughters who are relatively sympathetic or low in personal distress when exposed to another person who is distressed, and sympathetic fathers tend to have sympathetic sons. This pattern of findings could be due to children's modeling the ways that their parents deal with emotions or to the effects of sympathetic parenting on children's other-orientation, self-regulation skills, feelings about themselves and others, or other aspects of children's functioning (Dix, in press). Regardless of the mechanism involved, these findings are consistent with other data indicating that children who come from warm, supportive homes tend to be relatively empathic and prosocial (Barnett, 1987).

We also have obtained data indicating that the ways in which families deal with the expression of emotion are associated with people's vicariously induced emotional responding. In a study with adults, we found that individuals (primarily women) who came from homes in which positive emotions and subordinant negative emotions (for example, regret, sympathy) frequently were expressed reported relatively high levels of vicarious emotions (for example, sadness, sympathy, and distress) in reaction to viewing sympathy-inducing and distressing films (Eisenberg, Fabes, Schaller, Miller, and others, 1991). Moreover, we also found that parents' explicit reactions to children's emotional displays are associated with their sympathetic reactions. Parental reports of restrictiveness in regard to the general expression of emotions were associated with third- and sixth-grade children's facial distress (believed to be an index of personal distress) when recounting a sympathy-inducing experience (Eisenberg, Schaller, Fabes, and others, 1988).

In another study, we differentiated between restrictiveness in regard to the expression of emotions that can be hurtful to others (for example, staring at a disfigured person) and negative emotions unlikely to hurt others (for example, the child's own sadness or anxiety; Eisenberg, Fabes, Schaller, Carlo, and Miller, 1991). Self-reported, same-sex parental emphasis on controlling emotional displays that might hurt another was associated with elementary school children's self-reported dispositional and situational sympathy. In contrast, maternal emphasis on controlling emotions that were unlikely to injure another was associated with boys' facial and physiological signs of distress when viewing a sympathy-inducing film, as well as with self-reports of low distress in reaction to the film. Moreover, parental (primarily maternal) emphasis on emotional control (as assessed in an interview) was associated with low levels of sons' dispositional sympathy. Thus, parental emphasis on the control of hurtful emotional displays was associated with self-reported sympathy, whereas maternal emphasis on controlling the experience and display of self-related negative emotions was correlated with low sympathy and nonverbal indexes of personal distress for boys.

Parental teachings in regard to specific ways of dealing with one's own emotions also appear to be associated with children's tendency to experience sympathy. Parents (primarily mothers) who reported that they encouraged their children to deal instrumentally with sadness or anxiety had sons who exhibited less skin conductance arousal in response to a sympathy-inducing film (interpreted as an index of low personal distress) and were relatively high on situational and dispositional sympathy. Thus, parents who teach children to deal instrumentally with negative emotions and situations may be less likely to become overaroused with experiencing vicariously induced negative emotion and more likely to experience sympathy.

Socialization of Emotion and Ways of Responding to Others in Distress. In another study we examined the relation between mothers' reported emotion-related practices and young children's social behavior. Specifically, mothers of kindergarten and third-grade children were interviewed about what they typically do when their children are distressed or anxious, whether they overtly exhibit anxiety and sympathy themselves, and what their children do when they feel sorry for a peer. In addition, information regarding the expression of emotion in the home (Halberstadt, 1986) and restrictiveness versus lenience in regard to the expression of emotions that could hurt others (using a group of items from Saarni's [1985] scale) was obtained.

Mothers' reports of children's responses when they experienced sympathy were coded in several categories: (1) physically helps the other child deal with the problem or offers to do so (instrumental help), (2) talks with or comforts other child (but not explicit, physical assistance), (3) physically comforts (for example, hugs) other child, (4) nonverbally expresses concern for the other child but does not interact with him or her (for example, cries, looks sad or distressed), and (5) verbally expresses concern over the other child but does not interact with him or her. (The two categories "plays with child" and "does nothing" were used too infrequently to be included in the analyses.) Mothers' scores on a questionnaire measure of social desirability were unrelated to their reports of how their children responded when sympathizing.

For girls, attempts to provide instrumental assistance were significantly associated with the expression of submissive negative emotions (for example, regret, crying) in the home ($r[48] = .35, p < .01$), with mothers' self-reported tendencies to express overtly anxiety and sympathy ($r's[48] = .28$ and $.31, p's < .05$ and $.03$, respectively), and with maternal reinforcement of sympathy and prosocial behavior ($r[48] = .32, p < .03$). (All correlations are partial correlations, controlling for grade.) In contrast, the tendencies of mothers to focus on their children's own distress in sympathy-inducing situations (for example, to help the children understand their own sympathy) tended to be negatively associated with instrumental helping ($r[48] = -.24, p < .09$). In addition, for these relatively young children, maternal restrictiveness in regard to the expression of emotions that might hurt others (as assessed with a questionnaire) was inversely associated with instrumental helping ($r[48] = -.47, p < .001$).

Maternal restrictiveness in regard to hurtful emotional displays also was negatively associated with girls' talks with and comforting of the other child ($r[48] = -.35, p < .01$) and positively related to nonverbal expressions of sympathy but no physical assistance ($r[48] = .35, p < .02$). Moreover, paternal restrictiveness on the same index was associated with verbal sympathy but no physical assistance ($r[27] = .45, p < .02$) and was marginally, negatively related to talks with and comforting of the distressed peer ($r[27] = -.36, p < .06$), even though the sample of fathers was relatively small. Thus, it would appear that parental restrictiveness in regard to the expression of emotions, even hurtful emotions, may be associated with young girls' unwillingness or inability to behaviorally intervene when they feel sympathy for another.

There were relatively few significant relations for boys. However, consistent with the pattern of findings for girls, mothers' emphasis on their children's understanding of their own sympathy was related to children's nonverbal expressiveness but absence of physical action on the other child's behalf ($r[61] = .25, p < .05$). Moreover, as for daughters, mothers' tendencies to openly express their own anxiety was positively related to sons' instrumental helpfulness ($r[60] = .38, p < .005$). According to additional analyses, for sons only, paternal self-reported dispositional sympathy was positively related to instrumental helpfulness ($r[35] = .38, p < .02$).

In summary, these findings, albeit preliminary, suggest that socialization in the home affects not only how children respond emotionally to others' negative emotions but also how they react behaviorally. Overt expression of positive and negative submissive emotions in the home, maternal lenience in regard to the expression of emotion, and the reinforcement of sympathy and prosocial behavior seemed to be associated with young children's, particularly girls', instrumental helpfulness. In contrast, parental restrictiveness in regard to girls' emotional expressiveness was correlated with children's expressions of emotion, unaccompanied by action to alleviate the other's distress. These findings suggest that emotional expressivity in the home and reinforcement of emotional expressiveness may facilitate young girls' abilities to go beyond the mere expression of emotion to behavior designed to physically assist others. However, with increased age, parental restrictiveness rather than lenience in regard to the display of hurtful emotions may become more important in the development of children's sympathetic reactions (Eisenberg, Fabes, Schaller, Carlo, and Miller, 1991).

Socialization Correlates of Children's Social Competence, Popularity, and Coping with Emotion in Social Contexts. We have also been conducting research on children's reactions to their own and others' naturally occurring emotional reactions (Fabes, Eisenberg, McCormick, and Wilson, 1988). In our most current work, we are examining how children deal with their own negative emotions and the relation of their coping styles to social competence and popularity.

In one unpublished study, we have initial pilot data pertaining to the socialization correlates of preschoolers' methods of coping with their own anger. The children in this pilot study were three- to five-year-olds (nine boys and ten girls) who were in a larger study of anger and for whom we had parental data. Information about the ways in which they coped with anger was obtained using naturalistic observational procedures. Briefly, each day for three months at the study site, trained observers rotated systematically throughout the classrooms and playground and watched for any overt expression of anger by a child. When an overt anger expression was observed, the observer made brief notes regarding the anger reaction, the factors responsible for causing the anger, and how the angered child reacted to the provocation.

The reactions of the angered child were coded into one of six categories designed to identify the specific ways that the child attempted to cope with the anger conflict. The six coping categories included (1) revenge, or attempts to retaliate or get back at the provocateur with no other purpose evident (for example, hitting or threatening the provocateur), (2) active resistance, or attempts to defend one's position, possessions, or self-esteem in nonaggressive ways (for example, trying to get a toy back after it has been taken or telling someone to give it back), (3) venting, or expression of emotions without any action directed toward the provocateur or toward solving the conflict (for example, crying, sulking), (4) avoidance, or attempts to avoid or get away from the provocateur (for example, leaving the area to go play somewhere else), (5) adult seeking, or attempts or threats to go tell the teacher (for example, tattling) or to seek comfort from a teacher or other adult, and (6) expression of dislike, or tells the provocateur that he or she is not liked or cannot play because of what was done.

For every codable incident, each appropriate response category received a proportion score ranging from 0 (no reference to that category) to 1 (sole reference to that category). If more than one type of coping response was identified, each category was assigned a proportion score reflecting the relative proportion for a particular response category (for example, .5 for each of two responses).

Although the adaptiveness of a particular coping strategy varies depending on the given situation, in general avoidance and revenge responses are likely to be maladaptive, particularly if a social situation is controllable. Similarly, running to the teacher to tattle or for emotional support may not be very adaptive in the preschool setting, at least in regard to other children's reactions to the child. In contrast, the strategies of actively resisting and verbally asserting oneself and ostracizing the offending child (expression of dislike) may reflect social dominance and be relatively constructive responses. Indeed, in the larger sample, boys' expression of dislike and active resistance were significantly positively related to children's sociometric status, whereas girls' venting was negatively related. Moreover, revenge was negatively related to teachers' assessments of the children's social competence (for boys and girls; Fabes and Eisenberg, in press).

Teachers' assessments of children's social competence were obtained by having the children's teachers complete a six-item adaptation of Harter's (1979) Perceived Competence Scale for Children. Three items assessed children's abilities to make friends, and three items assessed their tendencies to act in socially appropriate ways. Teachers responded using a 4-point scale for which higher scores reflected greater social competence. Each child was rated by the two teachers (a primary teacher and an aide) who knew him or her the best, and the mean of the scores provided by both teachers was used in the analyses (reliability between raters for the larger sample was .70).

A positive-rating measure (using procedures similar to those used by Asher, Singleton, Tinsley, and Hymel, 1979) was used to assess sociometric status. Children indicated with whom they liked to play by sorting pictures of peers into three piles: (1) those with whom they liked to play "a little bit of the time" (this pile was marked by a picture of a neutral face), (2) those with whom they liked to play "some of the time" (marked by a small smile), and (3) those with whom they "really liked to play" (marked by a large smile). The nominations in the three piles were scored 0, 1, and 2, respectively; scores for each child were averaged. Thus, higher scores reflected greater sociometric status.

Parents' (mostly mothers') reactions to their children's negative emotions were assessed with a new scale, the Coping with Children's Negative Emotions Scale (CCNES; Fabes, Eisenberg, and Bernzweig, 1990). In the CCNES, parents were presented with twelve situations in which children are likely to experience distress and negative affect (for example, being teased by peers, being scared of injections, and being nervous about possibly embarrassing himself or herself in public); in none of the situations did the child's negative emotion have clear negative consequences for someone else. For each situation, parents were asked to indicate how likely (on a 7-point scale ranging from "very unlikely" to "very likely") they would be to react in each of six different alternative fashions. The six types of responses (CCNES subscales) included (1) distress reactions, reflecting the degree to which parents experience distress when children express negative affect (for example, "When my child becomes nervous, it makes me feel uncomfortable"), (2) punitive responses, reflecting the degree to which parents respond with punitive reactions that decrease their exposure to or need to deal with the negative emotions of their children (for example, "When my child becomes upset, I tell him [her] to straighten up or he [she] will have to go to his [her] room"), (3) emotional encouragement, reflecting the degree to which parents encourage children to express negative affect or validate their children's negative emotional states (for example, "When my child is on the verge of tears, I encourage him [her] to talk about his [her] feelings"), (4) emotion-focused responses, reflecting the degree to which parents respond with strategies that help the children feel better (for example, "When my child looks sad, I try to get him [her] to think about happy things"), (5) problem-focused responses, reflecting the degree to which parents help the children solve the problems that caused their distress (for example, "When my child becomes upset about breaking a prized possession, I help him [her] figure out how to get the possession fixed"), and (6) minimization responses, reflecting the degree to which parents minimize the seriousness of the situations or devalue the children's problems or distressed reactions (for example, "When my child becomes nervous, I tell him [her] that he [she] is making a big deal out of nothing").

The partial correlations (controlling for sex and age) between the parents' scores on the CCNES, the children's scores for frequency of becoming angry, and the children's various coping and social functioning categories are presented in Table 4.1. Although the sample was small, many correlations were at least marginally significant ($p < .10$). Because of the small number of subjects and the pilot nature of this study, findings significant at $p < .10$ or better are discussed here.

In general, the data supported the hypothesis that parental tactics that help the child deal with his or her own emotions or with the problem itself are positively related to coping and social competence, whereas parental practices that are punitive or devalue the child's emotional experiences are negatively related to adaptive styles of coping and social competence (at

Table 4.1. Partial Correlations Between Parents' Scores on CCNES Subscales and Children's Anger, Coping, and Social Functioning

Index	CCNES Subscales					
	MR	PR	EE	DR	PFR	EFR
Frequency of becoming angry[a]	.34[c]					-.35[c]
Coping responses						
Adult seeking		.37[c]	-.73[e]			
Revenge		.38[c]	-.55[d]		-.47[d]	-.40[c]
Avoidance		.41[c]		.43[c]		
Dislike				.37[c]	.37[c]	
Social functioning[b]						
Popularity			.33[c]		.37[c]	.33[c]
Social competence	-.48[d]					.44[d]

Note: Subscales of the Coping with Children's Negative Emotions Scale (CCNES): MR = minimization response; PR = punitive response; EE = emotional encouragement; DR = distress reactions; PFR = problem-focused responses; EFR = emotion-focused responses. Partial correlations were controlled for sex and age of children.

[a] df = 15
[b] df = 12
[c] $p < .10$
[d] $p < .05$
[e] $p < .001$

least as rated by teachers). Specifically, parental emphasis on problem-focused coping was negatively related to revenge and positively related to expression of dislike and children's popularity. Similarly, parental emphasis on emotion-focused coping (that helps the child feel better) was negatively related to revenge as well as the frequency of becoming angry, and positively related to both popularity and social competence. Parental encouragement of children's expression of emotion and validation of their emotional responses (emotional encouragement) also was associated with positive outcomes: low help seeking from adults, low revenge, and high popularity. Parental punitive responses, which would be expected to be associated with low levels of children's coping, were positively correlated with adult seeking revenge and avoidance. Moreover, parental minimization of the child's negative emotions was associated with high frequency of observed anger and low social competence. Finally, there was no clear pattern for parental distress reactions in response to children's negative emotions; this category of parental response was positively related to both avoidance and expression of dislike. Children's active resistance and venting were unrelated to parental responses.

Given the relatively small number of children in this pilot study, the aforementioned data should be viewed as suggestive. Nonetheless, overall the data suggest that parental practices that help children learn instrumental ways of dealing with negative situations and ways of managing their own negative emotions also help children learn to cope adaptively with anger. In contrast, parental punitive reactions and minimization of children's negative emotions were associated with negative outcomes. As suggested by Buck (1984), children who receive sanctions for the expression of their negative emotions are likely to hide their feelings while experiencing relatively high levels of physiological arousal. Thus, they are likely to become overaroused and engage in inappropriate behaviors. Moreover, if their parents are not understanding in regard to their children's feelings, children may learn to react negatively to others' negative emotions and may not learn supportive ways of responding to others.

Summary

We have proposed that how children deal with emotional arousal in social situations affects the quality of their social interactions. More specifically, we have argued that children who can regulate negative emotions so that they are not overly aroused interact in more adaptive ways. Based on these assumptions, we have started to examine the relations of parental characteristics and practices to children's emotional responding and social behavior. Initial research findings provide partial support for the conclusion that parental encouragement of children's expression of their own sadness, distress, and sympathy, as well as parental practices that teach children ways to deal with negative emotion-eliciting situations and their own negative emotions, are associated with sympathetic emotional responding and with adaptive social behavior. These findings suggest that further examination of the ways in which children learn to manage their emotions in social interactions will serve to augment our understanding of the socialization of social competence.

References

Asher, S. R., Singleton, L. C., Tinsley, B. R., and Hymel, S. "A Reliable Sociometric Measure for Preschool Children." *Developmental Psychology,* 1979, *15,* 443-444.
Barnett, M. A. "Empathy and Related Responses in Children." In N. Eisenberg and J. Strayer (eds.), *Empathy and Its Development.* Cambridge, England: Cambridge University Press, 1987.
Buck, R. *The Communication of Emotion.* New York: Guilford, 1984.
Camras, L. A. "Facial Expression Used by Children in a Conflict Situation." *Child Development,* 1977, *48,* 1431-1435.

Carlson, M., and Miller, N. "Explanation of the Relation Between Negative Mood and Helping." *Psychological Bulletin*, 1987, *102*, 91-108.

Coie, J. D., Dodge, K. A., and Kupersmidt, J. B. "Peer Group Behavior and Social Status." In S. R. Asher and J. D. Coie (eds.), *Peer Rejection in Childhood*. Cambridge, England: Cambridge University Press, 1990.

Cummings, E. M., and Cummings, J. L. "A Process-Oriented Approach to Children's Coping with Adults' Angry Behavior." *Developmental Review*, 1988, *8*, 296-321.

Denham, S. A. "Social Cognition, Prosocial Behavior, and Emotion in Preschoolers: Contextual Validation." *Child Development*, 1986, *57*, 194-201.

Derryberry, D., and Rothbart, M. K. "Arousal, Affect, and Attention as Components of Temperament." *Journal of Personality and Social Psychology*, 1988, *55*, 958-966.

Dix, T. "Parenting on Behalf of the Child: Empathic Goals in the Regulation of Responsive Parenting." In I. E. Sigel, A. V. McGillicuddy-DeLisi, and J. J. Goodnow (eds.), *Parental Belief Systems: The Psychological Consequences for Children*. Vol. 2. Hillsdale, N.J.: Erlbaum, in press.

Dunn, J., Bretherton, I., and Munn, P. "Conversations About Feeling States Between Mothers and Their Young Children." *Developmental Psychology*, 1987, *23*, 132-139.

Eisenberg, N., Bernzweig, J., and Fabes, R. A. "Coping and Vicarious Emotional Responding." In T. Field, P. McCabe, and N. Schneiderman (eds.), *Stress and Coping in Childhood*. Hillsdale, N.J.: Erlbaum, 1992.

Eisenberg, N., Cameron, E., Tryon, K., and Dodez, R. "Socialization of Prosocial Behavior in the Preschool Classroom." *Developmental Psychology*, 1981, *17*, 773-782.

Eisenberg, N., and Fabes, R. A. "Prosocial Behavior and Empathy: A Multimethod, Developmental Perspective." In P. S. Clark (ed.), *Review of Personality and Social Psychology*. Vol. 12. Newbury Park, Calif.: Sage, 1991.

Eisenberg, N., Fabes, R. A., Miller, P. A., Shell, C., Shea, R., May-Plumee, T. "Preschoolers' Vicarious Emotional Responding and Their Situational and Dispositional Prosocial Behavior." *Merrill-Palmer Quarterly*, 1990, *36*, 507-529.

Eisenberg, N., Fabes, R. A., Schaller, M., Carlo, G., and Miller, P. A. "The Relations of Parental Characteristics and Practices to Children's Vicarious Emotional Responding." *Child Development*, 1991, *62*, 1393-1408.

Eisenberg, N., Fabes, R. A., Schaller, M., Miller, P. A., Carlo, G., Poulin, R., Shea, C., and Shell, R. "Personality and Socialization Correlates of Vicarious Emotional Responding." *Journal of Personality and Social Psychology*, 1991, *61*, 459-470.

Eisenberg, N., McCreath, H., and Ahn, R. "Vicarious Emotional Responsiveness and Prosocial Behavior: Their Interrelations in Young Children." *Personality and Social Psychology Bulletin*, 1988, *14*, 298-311.

Eisenberg, N., Pasternack, J. F., Cameron, E., and Tryon, K. "The Relation of Quantity and Mode of Prosocial Behavior to Moral Cognitions and Social Style." *Child Development*, 1984, *55*, 1479-1485.

Eisenberg, N., Schaller, M., Fabes, R. A., Bustamante, D., Mathy, R., Shell, R., and Rhodes, K. "The Differentiation of Personal Distress and Sympathy in Children and Adults." *Developmental Psychology*, 1988, *24*, 766-775.

Eisenberg-Berg, N., and Hand, M. "The Relationship of Preschoolers' Reasoning About Prosocial Moral Conflicts to Prosocial Behavior." *Child Development*, 1979, *50*, 356-363.

Fabes, R. A., and Eisenberg, N. "Young Children's Coping with Interpersonal Anger." *Child Development*, in press.

Fabes, R. A., Eisenberg, N., and Bernzweig, J. "The Coping with Children's Negative Emotions Scale: Description and Scoring." Unpublished manuscript, Department of Family Resources and Human Development, Arizona State University, 1990.

Fabes, R. A., Eisenberg, N., McCormick, S. E., and Wilson, M. S. "Preschoolers' Attributions of the Situational Determinants of Others' Naturally Occurring Emotions." *Developmental Psychology*, 1988, *24*, 376-385.

Fabes, R. A., Eisenberg, N., and Miller, P. A. "Maternal Correlates of Children's Vicarious Emotional Responsiveness." *Developmental Psychology*, 1990, *26*, 639–648.

Fox, N. A. "Psychophysiological Correlates of Emotional Reactivity During the First Year of Life." *Developmental Psychology*, 1989, *25*, 364–372.

Gottman, J. M., and Katz, L. F. "Effects of Marital Discord on Young Children's Peer Interaction and Health." *Developmental Psychology*, 1989, *25*, 373–381.

Halberstadt, A. G. "Family Socialization of Emotional Expression and Nonverbal Communication Styles and Skills." *Journal of Personality and Social Psychology*, 1986, *51*, 827–836.

Harter, S. *Perceived Competence Scale for Children: Manual.* Denver, Colo.: University of Denver, 1979.

Hoffman, M. L. "Altruistic Behavior and the Parent-Child Relationship." *Journal of Personality and Social Psychology*, 1975, *31*, 937–943.

Hoffman, M. L. "Development of Prosocial Motivation: Empathy and Guilt." In N. Eisenberg (ed.), *The Development of Prosocial Behavior*. San Diego, Calif.: Academic Press, 1982.

Kopp, C. B. "Regulation of Distress and Negative Emotions: A Developmental View." *Developmental Psychology*, 1989, *25*, 343–354.

Larrieu, J. A. "Prosocial Values, Assertiveness, and Sex: Predictors of Children's Naturalistic Helping." Paper presented at the biennial meeting of the Southwestern Society for Research in Human Development, Denver, Colorado, March 1984.

Larsen, R. J., Diener, E., and Cropanzano, R. A. "Cognitive Operations Associated with Individual Differences in Affect Intensity." *Journal of Personality and Social Psychology*, 1987, *53*, 767–774.

Lazarus, R. S., and Folkman, S. *Stress, Appraisal, and Coping.* New York: Springer, 1984.

Lewis, M., and Michalson, L. *Children's Emotions and Moods.* New York: Plenum, 1983.

Malatesta, C. Z., and Haviland, J. M. "Signals, Symbols, and Socialization: The Modification of Emotional Expression in Human Development." In M. Lewis and C. Saarni (eds.), *The Socialization of Emotions*. New York: Plenum, 1985.

Mehrabian, A. *Basic Dimensions for a General Psychological Theory.* Cambridge, Mass.: Oelgeschlager, Gunn, and Hain, 1980.

Parker, J. G., and Asher, S. R. "Peer Relations and Later Personal Adjustment: Are Low-Accepted Children at Risk?" *Psychological Bulletin*, 1987, *102*, 357–389.

Radke-Yarrow, M., and Zahn-Waxler, C. "Roots, Motives, and Patterns in Children's Prosocial Behavior." In E. Staub, D. Bar-Tal, J. Karylowski, and J. Reykowski (eds.), *Development and Maintenance of Prosocial Behavior: International Perspectives on Positive Behavior*. New York: Plenum, 1984.

Roberts, W., and Strayer, J. "Parents' Responses to the Emotional Distress of Their Children: Relations with Children's Social Competence." *Developmental Psychology*, 1987, *23*, 414–422.

Rothbart, M. K., and Derryberry, D. "Development of Individual Differences in Temperament." In M. E. Lamb and A. L. Brown (eds.), *Advances in Developmental Psychology*. Vol. 1. Hillsdale, N.J.: Erlbaum, 1981.

Saarni, C. "Indirect Processes in Affect Socialization." In M. Lewis and C. Saarni (eds.), *The Socialization of Emotions*. New York: Plenum, 1985.

Thomas, A., Chess, S., and Birch, H. *Temperament and Behavior Disorders in Children.* New York: New York University Press, 1968.

Wood, J. V., Saltzberg, J. A., and Goldsamt, L. A. "Does Affect Induce Self-Focused Attention?" *Journal of Personality and Social Psychology*, 1990, *58*, 899–908.

Wood, J. V., Saltzberg, J. A., Neale, J. N., Stone, A. A., and Rachmiel, T. B. "Self-Focused Attention, Coping Responses, and Distressed Mood in Everyday Life." *Journal of Personality and Social Psychology*, 1990, *58*, 1027–1036.

Nancy Eisenberg *is Regents' Professor of psychology at Arizona State University.*

Richard A. Fabes *is associate professor in the Department of Family Resources and Human Development at Arizona State University.*

Gustavo Carlo *is a graduate student in the Department of Psychology at Arizona State University.*

Mariss Karbon *is a graduate student in the Department of Family Resources and Human Development at Arizona State University.*

Childrens' affective reactions to others' emotionally expressive cues change with development and individual variation in children's resources to cope with the situation.

Children's Affective Responses to the Expressive Cues of Others

Daphne Blunt Bugental, Victoria Cortez, Jay Blue

In this chapter, we are concerned with developmental change and individual variation in the ways in which children come to use expressive information from others. In particular, we are interested in children's responses to social cues to potential threat or danger, as presaged by the negative expressive behavior of others. To what extent does the witnessed affect of others influence children's internal regulatory processes? To what extent do children respond with direct emotional contagion and mobilization for defensive action as opposed to deployment of cognitive resources? And to what extent do such variations in internal regulatory processes influence memory processes?

The expressive behavior of others provides a rich, ongoing source of information as to probable future events. The facial expressions of others may signal the future course of their behavior as well as indirectly provide information about the environment. Expressed fear, for example, not only signals the possibility that the expressor will withdraw from a situation but also suggests that the situation may contain threat. Thus, the expressive behavior of others can be thought of as an early warning system that provides probabilistic information about future events in uncertain or ambiguous situations.

This research was supported by a grant from the National Institute of Mental Health (5 R01 MH39095) and a grant from the National Science Foundation. We express our appreciation to Hal Kopeikin and Jeff Lewis, who provided the programming assistance needed for this study and made substantive contributions throughout the project.

The welfare of the individual with low strategic resources to cope with threat is best served by a response system that immediately and automatically facilitates escape to safety when there are cues of danger. The welfare of more competent individuals is best served by a response system that fosters broad attentional deployment and easy access to cognitive resources. Thus, it can be anticipated that effective response systems will change with social cognitive development and experience. Up until now, the adaptiveness of response patterns to the expressive cues of others has focused either on infancy or adulthood. In this chapter, we focus on changes that occur across middle childhood—a period of rapid transition in social information-processing skills.

We expected that younger children (who have relatively low social processing skills, low cultural knowledge about communication rules, and low competence to influence their environment) respond to social cues of threat with a coordinated pattern of autonomic mobilization and simplified cognitive activity. Such "automatic" response patterns provide optimum access to overlearned cognitive structures (for example, scripts) and readiness for action. In contrast, older children (who have higher levels of social processing skill, emergent cultural knowledge about communication rules, and enhanced social power in their environment) were expected to react to expressive cues of potential threat with increasing levels of attention and controlled processing of contextual information. This pattern maximizes the possibilities for information acquisition and flexible response patterns. In discussing automatic versus controlled processing, we are borrowing constructs from cognitive psychology (Shiffrin and Schneider, 1977). Although this distinction has received considerable attention in social psychology (for example, Bargh, 1982), it has not as yet been well incorporated into the social developmental literature.

In this chapter, we are concerned with individual and age-related variations in processing of expressive cues. We anticipated that children who have low perceived social control are particularly dependent on expressive cues of others as sources of influence on their response styles. Children who see themselves as having relatively low power in their interpersonal contacts may be more likely to rely on the cues offered by others than to rely on their own interpretive processes. Thus, we predicted parallels between the processing patterns of younger children and the processing patterns of individuals with low perceived control.

Responses to the Expressed Affect of Others

At all ages, the affect expressed by others may potentially act as the basis for emotional contagion, information-processing changes, and/or behavioral action. These responses are particularly likely in relation to ambiguous or uncertain environmental events. The expressed affect of others acts as a strong stimulus for matched observer responses. Additionally, witnessed or experienced affect may be thought of as both limiting and selectively directing cognitive processes—as well as being influenced by them.

Emotional contagion effects have been observed, in general, across the life span. Shortly after birth, infants will cry in response to tape-recorded cries of other infants (Sagi and Hoffman, 1976), and within a few months they respond reciprocally to the expressed behavior of caregivers (for example, Lelwica and Haviland, 1983). Emotional contagion continues into adulthood. For example, Vaughn and Lanzetta (1980) found evidence of emotional contagion in response to the witnessed distress of others; and Howes, Hokanson, and Lowenstein (1985) demonstrated that manifestations of depressed affect may induce parallel effects in others. Hsee, Hatfield, Carlson, and Chemtob (1990) documented the extent to which the witnessed affect of others—both happiness and sadness—induces parallel affective responses in observers within a laboratory setting.

Early concern with cognitive responses to the expressed affect of others emerged as an offshoot of the social comparison literature. Schachter (1959) demonstrated that adults are more likely to seek the company of others when confronted with an expected threatening event (mild electric shocks). Not only can association with others under these circumstances serve to alleviate distress, but also the responses of others can provide comparative information regarding interpretation of and appropriate emotional response to the potential threat. As this line of research developed, it became clear that such social referencing processes were more probable in situations in which the other person had important similarities to the observer, for example, the experience of an equivalent level of threat (Zimbardo and Formica, 1963).

Subsequently, interest turned to changes in information-processing patterns as a function of the individual's *own* affective state. Affective states have been associated with reductions in processing capacity (for example, Ellis, Thomas, and Rodriguez, 1984), biased access to memory (Bower, 1981), selective encoding processes (for example, Teasdale and Fogarty, 1979), and greater use of heuristics in processing patterns (for example, Isen and Daubman, 1984). The effects of positive and negative affect do not, however, appear to be completely symmetrical (Isen, 1984). As an oversimplification, positive affect—typically associated with moderate levels of arousal (for example, Levenson, Ekman, and Friesen, 1990)—often leads to enhanced processing; it may also, however, lead to greater use of heuristics (Isen and Daubman, 1984). Negative affect—often associated with higher and suboptimal levels of arousal—has been found to more regularly lead to disruptions in cognitive processing (for example, Leight and Ellis, 1981; Hasher and Zacks, 1979).

Less is known about changes in information processing as a function of witnessing the effect of others. Research by Hertel and Narvaez (1986) has suggested that direct observation of the affect of others may in general lead to impairment in memory for associated semantic content.

Transitions Across Middle Childhood. Within developmental psychology, most of our attention has focused on the ways in which *infants and young children* react to emotional cues from others. Infants respond to the affect shown by others as a basis for both their own emotional reactions and their behavioral responses to ambiguous events (Klinnert and others, 1983; Cohn and Tronick, 1983). As Barrett and Campos (1987) have argued, witnessing of the emotional reactions of others provides meaning or significance to ambiguous events.

During their early years, children are likely to respond to the emotions of others as if they themselves were experiencing the witnessed states (Hoffman, 1977). For this reason, expressed negative affect by others may directly influence the processing patterns shown by the child who observes such affect. For example, Cummings's research has shown that witnessed affect may have negative consequences for young children, even when it is not directed toward them (Cummings and Cummings, 1988; El-Sheikh, Cummings, and Goetsch, 1989).

With the increased inferential and integrative abilities of middle childhood—in concert with expanded social experience and cultural knowledge—a greater number of options become available in response to the witnessed affect of others. At younger ages, children's inferences regarding the inner states of others are primarily influenced by surface appearances; that is, the person who has a happy facial expression is interpreted as experiencing a happy state, even when counterinformation is available and understood (Livesley and Bromley, 1973). But with expanding awareness of the role of intentions and potential discrepancies between inner and outer states, children's responses to witnessed affect become less automatic. In making inferences regarding the inner states of others, children increasingly use relevant information regarding the personal history of others or the contextual forces operating in the situation—in addition to the other person's expressed affect (Gnepp and Gould, 1985; Hoffner and Badzinski, 1989; Reichenbach and Masters, 1983). Moreover, these children are acquiring knowledge of social rules about expressed affect, and the extent to which such rules may dictate behavior that is inconsistent with experienced reactions (Saarni, 1979, 1984). As children come to understand that expressive responses can be deliberately manipulated in the service of social goals, they give increasing weight to alternative information that provides a *contextual* explanation for witnessed affect. And in doing so, they may be less prone to direct contagion effects and better able to use the expressive cues of others as probabilistic signals about the state of that individual or about other ongoing events.

Individual Differences. Just as the younger child places higher reliance on environmental cues than does the older child, and shows greater reactivity to potential stressors than does the older child, there may be variability at all ages in the interpretive use of expressive cues in the social environment. Perceived social control may provide an important source of individual variability in responses given to the expressive behavior of others. If a child comes to believe that he or she has relatively low control in the social environment, the child may show higher reactivity not only to potential sources of threat but also to the cues of others in determining an appropriate response to social stimuli.

The adult literature on perceived control as a moderator of response to stress and to social influence has a long history. By now, it is apparent that coping strategies (for example, use of emotion-focused versus problem-focused strategies; Lazarus and Folkman, 1984) may vary as a function of perceived control. Individuals who tend to see themselves as lacking control in their environment may react more intensely and less adaptively to stressors; conversely, individuals who believe that they have high control in their environment are less likely to show negative reactions to stressors (for example, Abramson, Seligman, and Teasdale, 1978; Lefcourt, Miller, Ware, and Sherk, 1981; Phares, 1976; Sacks and Bugental, 1987). Research conducted within our own laboratory has focused on the maladaptive reactions of adults with low perceived control to the potential stress induced by "difficult" children (for example, Bugental, Blue, and Lewis, 1990; Bugental and Shennum, 1984).

The ways in which a given child processes a potential threat will vary with his or her history and with the appraisal of the immediate situation. Children whose "social scripts" or "working models" (Bowlby, 1969) of interpersonal relationships assign a relatively weak or powerless role to self can be expected to be more reactive to expressive cues from others, and to deploy defensive resources in a different way from that of children whose social scripts assign a powerful role to self. In conducting the research described below on children's responses to the expressed affect of others in fear-inducing settings, we anticipated that children who believe that they have low control within interpersonal relationships would show greater processing deficits (for example, memory errors and use of heuristics) in response to cues to threat than would children with higher levels of perceived control.

Studies on Child Responses to the Expressed Affect of Others in Fear-Inducing Settings

Study 1: Differences in Processing Styles as a Function of Age and Perceived Social Control

In our first set of studies, children were exposed to stimulus materials (a videotape of a child having a medical exam) that were potentially fear inducing. Children were preselected for differences in age and control perceptions and were randomly assigned to our experimental conditions (age effects received attention in Bugental and others, in press; perceived control effects are reported in detail within this chapter). Children viewed videotapes in which the affect expressed facially by actors was either positive, neutral, or negative. Continuous records were made of children's autonomic responses (heart rate and skin conductance level) during these procedures. Additionally, measures were later taken of their memory for witnessed events.

Method. Children between the ages of five and ten (N = 120) were brought to our laboratory on two separate occasions. On the first occasion, they were given a picture attribution test (PIXAT). This instrument was designed to assess children's attributions regarding the reasons for problems and solutions in family interactions. Children are asked to tell stories in connection with four sets of pictures that involve a "problem" and a "solution." For example, the problem picture might show a parent spanking a child, and the solution picture might show a parent hugging a child. Children select from a series of cartoon pictures to explain the events that led up to the problem, and then they select from a second set of cartoon pictures to explain the events that led to the solution. For purposes of this study (with the focus on potential problems), pictures selected as problem "causes" were employed as indexes of the child's perceived control over social problems.

All pictures used in the PIXAT have been prescored for perceived controllability of depicted events. That is, a child with a high "child-controllability" score might select pictures in which a child is shown engaging in a naughty act (an event given a high rating for child controllability by adult judges); alternatively, a child with a low child-controllability score might select pictures in which the child is sick, the weather is bad, or the parent has a bad day (all rated as relatively uncontrollable).

Scoring in the present study was limited to the first three problem pictures selected in each story. Tests were used only for those children who used at least two problem pictures in telling each story. Using Cronbach's alpha to provide an estimate of reliability across picture pairs, we obtained a coefficient of .74 for child-controllability scores. Reliability estimates for adult-controllability scores did not reach significance. For this reason, attributional scores were limited to the child-controllability dimension. It should be noted that perceived control scores were unrelated to age (r = .14).

Children watched a videotape of a seven-year-old boy having a routine medical exam. We obtained advance measures of young children's scripts about a visit to the doctor; this information then formed the basis for depicted events. In some cases, the events shown were *consistent* with children's scripts (for example, the doctor used a stethoscope to listen to the child's chest), whereas other events *violated* children's scripts (for example, the doctor offered the child a prize before he examined him).

We measured children's recall of witnessed events at a later time by asking them both free and cued recall questions about the videotape material. We assessed two types of processing errors: (1) script-consistent errors, that is, false recall of events that usually occur in a medical examination (for example, "recalling" that the child received a shot when in fact he did not) and (2) script-irrelevant errors, for example, recall of general information of an "unscripted" nature such as the child's name. The first type of error suggests reliance on heuristics; the second type of error suggests interference with the acquisition of new information.

Results and Discussion. Our analyses of age effects and attributional effects on processing efficiency follow.

Age Effects on Processing Efficiency. In the first analysis, we measured children's memory errors as a function of their age and the affective cues in the videotape (happy, fearful, or neutral cues from the child actor). As expected, there was a significant interaction between these variables (Bugental and others, in press). The youngest age group (age five to age six) was most likely to show errors after watching a tape containing expressive cues to negative affect (in comparison with neutral or positive affect). Conversely, children in the oldest age group (age nine to age ten) manifested the greatest accuracy after watching a tape containing expressive cues to negative affect (seven- and eight-year-old children did not show any systematic differences in response to stimulus cues). The same pattern of effects was found for both script-consistent and script-irrelevant errors.

The youngest children also showed immediate heart rate elevation in response to the witnessed fear of another child (no significant differences were found in response to affect displayed by the doctor at another time). These elevations in turn acted as predictors of subsequent processing errors. Among older age groups, heart rate levels were slightly (but nonsignificantly) lower in the negative than in the neutral condition; heart rate levels were, however, unrelated to error frequency.

In summary, children manifested different processing patterns in response to the expressive cues of others as a function of their age. Younger children showed correlated patterns of autonomic arousal and memory deficit in response to witnessing a fear-arousing event. Conversely, older children showed no adverse autonomic reactions and evidenced enhanced accuracy in response to fear cues. This developmental shift is subject to alternative interpretations. The level of threat posed by a seven-year-old child depicting a fear response may have been greater to a five- to six-year-old than it was to a nine- to ten-year-old, thus leading to more disruptive levels of arousal for younger children. It should be noted, however, that older children reported that, if anything, they would feel higher levels of distress than were reported by younger children in response to the negative expressive cues witnessed.

If, in fact, equivalent levels of distress were experienced by both age groups, differences in response patterns may have reflected differences in affect regulation processes. The immediate heart rate acceleration shown by younger children in response to the fearful affect of another child suggests a contagion response. This response is adaptive for an individual preparing to engage in physical action such as flight. Conversely, the steady heart rate shown by older children may provide an optimum state for information acquisition.

Attributional Effects on Processing Efficiency. In a second analysis, children were divided into two groups: those with high versus those with low perceived control. A multivariate analysis of variance was conducted to assess the script-consistent and script-irrelevant errors as a function of three variables: age, valence of witnessed affect, and perceived child control (median split). A significant main effect was obtained for perceived child control ($F[4,70] = 4.63$, $p < .04$). Additionally, significant interactions were obtained between type of error and perceived control ($F[2,70] = 3.61$, $p < .04$) and between type of error, age, and valence of witnessed affect ($F[4,70] = 2.63$, $p < .04$).

A separate follow-up analysis of script-consistent errors revealed a main effect for perceived child control ($F[1,70] = 4.48$, $p < .04$); children with low perceived control showed a higher overall level of script-consistent errors ($M = 2.15$) than did children with high perceived control ($M = 1.63$), suggesting that low-control children may have a greater tendency to rely on heuristics (cultural scripts for such events) in processing potentially threatening information. A separate follow-up analysis of script-irrelevant errors revealed a significant interaction between perceived child control and witnessed affect ($F[1,70] = 3.38$, $p < .04$). As shown in Figure 5.1, children with low perceived control showed a high level of errors in the negative condition (relative to the positive and neutral conditions), whereas children with high perceived control showed a comparatively low level of errors in the negative condition. No significant autonomic effects were found in response to expressive cues of actors as a function of perceived control of subjects.

Differences in information processing as a function of perceived control parallel those found as a function of age. For example, children with low perceived control (at all ages) were negatively reactive to cues to threat. When they witnessed a negative facial display, they showed decreased accuracy in acquiring new information; that is, they made a larger number of errors in recalling witnessed events than did low-control children who witnessed neutral or positive expressive cues. Conversely, children with high perceived control manifested increased processing accuracy in response to expressive cues to threat. When they witnessed a negative facial display, they showed relatively high accuracy in acquiring new information; that is, they made a smaller number of errors in recalling script-irrelevant information than did high-control children who witnessed neutral or positive affect.

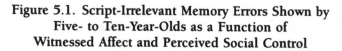

Figure 5.1. Script-Irrelevant Memory Errors Shown by
Five- to Ten-Year-Olds as a Function of
Witnessed Affect and Perceived Social Control

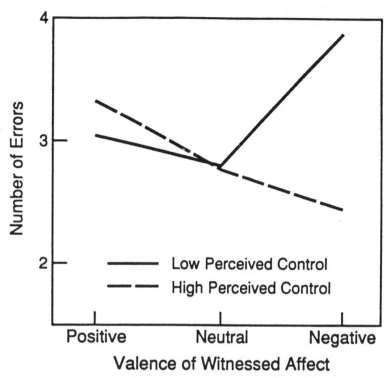

But there were also important differences between age effects and attributional effects. For example, the differences observed as a function of perceived control did not appear to be mediated by autonomic processes. Additionally, there was a general pattern for children with low perceived control to make greater use of heuristics in processing; that is, they made significantly more errors that were consistent with scripted accounts of the witnessed event but inconsistent with events actually seen.

It is probable that there are multiple pathways for interference with processing efficiency in response to expressive cues to threat. The first pathway is mediated by autonomic arousal. This is the pathway more typical for cognitively immature children as a whole. The high levels of autonomic reactivity of younger children may reflect the extent to which these children are more directly influenced by expressive cues of others, which in turn acts to mediate cognitive deficits. A second possible pathway is mediated by variations in cognitive processing patterns. Children with low perceived control may show deficient processing by virtue of cognitions triggered by schema activation. Once social cues are present to support the activation of a social threat schema (more accessible for individuals with low perceived control), these children may subsequently show deficits in their ability to acquire new information.

Study 2: Experimental Induction of Processing Competence

The first study addressed the issue of naturally occurring differences among children in the extent to which they showed processing changes in response to witnessed affect. These control perceptions were conceptualized as having direct consequences for information-processing patterns. Alternatively, of course, control perceptions may simply serve as markers of other individual differences among children, for example, temperament differences. In order to test the *causal* influence of control perceptions, we conducted a second investigation that employed a priming manipulation.

A second group of children were experimentally primed for different levels of control *before* witnessing the doctor videotape (Cortez, 1991). The experimental procedures employed represent an extension of those used in Study 1. Because the strongest deficits in response to witnessed negative affect were shown by the youngest age group in Study 1, Study 2 was limited to five- and six-year-old children. Additionally, witnessed affect was limited to negative versus neutral affect because no consistent differences were found in Study 1 between responses shown to neutral versus positive affect. In Study 2, half of the children were primed for "child control" in advance of seeing the doctor videotape, and half of the children were primed for "adult control" in advance of seeing the tape. The priming manipulation consisted of showing subjects videotaped depictions of fairy tales in which either a child or a parent was the hero who "saved the day" in comparable dilemmas.

As reported elsewhere (Cortez, 1991), priming was found to have consequences for information-processing patterns shown in response to the doctor videotape. An initial analysis revealed different patterns for script-consistent versus script-irrelevant errors. Significant priming effects were only observed for script-irrelevant errors, that is, for the acquisition of new information. As can be seen in Figure 5.2, the effects of priming were limited to the condition in which children witnessed affective cues to potential threat (a fearful child actor). In the neutral condition, advance priming had no discernible consequences for processing errors. But in the condition in which children witnessed a fearful child, priming had consequences that paralleled those observed for children's initial levels of perceived control. That is, children who were primed for high *adult* control over a negative event showed low processing accuracy after witnessing negative expressive cues on the doctor videotape. Conversely, children who were primed for high *child* control over a negative event showed relatively high processing efficiency after witnessing negative expressive cues on the doctor videotape.

Figure 5.2. Script-Irrelevant Memory Errors Shown by
Five- and Six-Year-Olds as a Function of Witnessed Affect and
Experimentally Primed Social Control

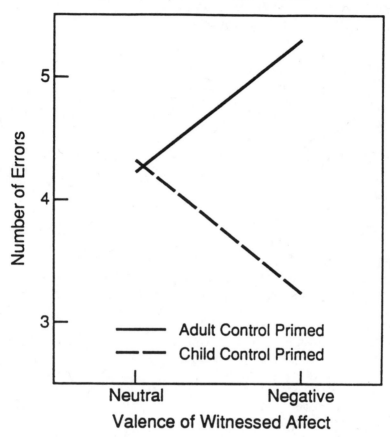

Integration and Summary of Findings

In conclusion, it appears that processing deficits in response to expressive
cues to threat are more probable for younger children and/or for children
with low perceived control. Before the age of seven, children were more
likely to respond with the coordinated response pattern of increased autonomic arousal and decreased cognitive efficiency in response to fear cues
shown by another child. At later ages, these same cues more commonly led
to cognitive vigilance and accurate processing—a more adaptive response
as the observer's competencies increase.

Across the years of age five to age ten, there were also individual
differences among children in processing patterns in response to potential

threat. Children with low perceived control showed processing deficits that paralleled those shown by younger children. In both groups, processing accuracy decreased after witnessing expressive cues to threat. In contrast, older children and children with higher levels of perceived control responded to expressive cues to threat with increased processing accuracy.

Low-control perceptions appear to act in a causal fashion to produce processing deficits. That is, the same general pattern of errors in information acquisition (script-irrelevant information) was shown by children who were experimentally primed for low control as by children with initially low perceptions of control. In both groups, deficiencies were shown in delayed memory for events that were associated with expressive cues to threat. Conversely, children with initially high perceptions of control manifested processing patterns that closely matched those shown by children who were primed for high levels of child control. In both groups, increases in processing accuracy in the acquisition of new information were shown in response to witnessing negative expressive cues (in comparison with witnessing neutral affect).

The processing deficits shown by children with low perceived control did not appear to be mediated by changes in autonomic levels, however. It will be necessary in the future to determine the different mediating processes that characterize children with different social attributional patterns. In ongoing companion research with adults, for example, we have observed that threat-focused ideation (for example, thoughts about the characteristics of the other person that might interfere with pleasant interaction) is more common for individuals with low perceived control; such ideation appears to precede dysfunctional communication processes (Bugental, 1991). Since we did not obtain any measures of the ongoing thoughts of children during the present study, we can only conjecture about the cognitive processes underlying our data. It may be that potential threat elicits threat-focused ideation among children with low expected control; information-processing errors would, in turn, reflect the disruptive role of such interfering thoughts.

A final question concerns the functionality of the observed regulatory processes. The general course of developmental change in response to witnessed affect can be seen as potentially functional with respect to the child's increasing competencies. Reliance on the expressive cues of others is functionally adaptive for infants and younger children. But as the child acquires social-cognitive capacities and social knowledge, reduction in exclusive reliance on the expressive cues of others is also adaptive. The relative advantages of variations in reactivity as a function of differences in perceived control are more doubtful—in particular, among older children who have comparatively greater social knowledge and processing capacity to bring to bear on the interpretive process. Reliance on the expressive cues of others—more common among children with low perceived control—offers a short-term advantage for socially "dependent" individuals in that such cues offer a prepackaged explanation of witnessed events and a suggested behavioral course. But these automatic processing patterns can be expected to be dysfunctional on a long-term basis. Reliance on these mechanisms ultimately interferes with accurate processing and limits the possibilities for flexible responses to changing social contexts. Children who maintain this processing dependence can reasonably be expected to show continuing deficits in their ability to process new information in the presence of cues to threat.

References

Abramson, L. Y., Seligman, M.E.P., and Teasdale, J. D. "Learned Helplessness in Humans: Critique and Reformulation." *Psychological Review,* 1978, *96,* 358–372.

Bargh, J. A. "Automatic and Conscious Processing of Social Information." In R. S. Wyer, Jr., and T. K. Srull (eds.), *Handbook of Social Cognition.* Vol. 3. Hillsdale, N.J.: Erlbaum, 1982.

Barrett, K. C., and Campos, J. J. "Perspectives on Emotional Development. Part 2: A Functionalist Approach to Emotions." In J. D. Osofsky (ed.), *Handbook of Infant Development.* New York: Wiley, 1987.

Bower, G. "Mood and Memory." *American Psychologist,* 1981, *36,* 129–148.

Bowlby, J. *Attachment and Loss.* Vol. 1. New York: Basic Books, 1969.

Bugental, D. B. "Adult Processing Deficits in Stressful Caregiving Interactions." Paper presented at the biennial meeting of the Society for Research in Child Development, Seattle, Washington, April 1991.

Bugental, D. B., Blue, J., Cortez, V., Fleck, K., and Rodriguez, A. "Influences of Witnessed Affect on Information Processing in Children." *Child Development,* in press.

Bugental, D. B., Blue, J., and Lewis, J. "Caregiver Cognitions as Moderators of Affective Reactions to 'Difficult' Children." *Developmental Psychology,* 1990, *26,* 631–638.

Bugental, D. B., and Shennum, W. A. *"Difficult" Children as Elicitors and Targets of Adult Communication Patterns: An Attributional-Behavioral Transactional Analysis.* Monographs of the Society for Research in Child Development, vol. 49, no. 1 (serial no. 205). Chicago: University of Chicago Press, 1984.

Cohn, J., and Tronick, E. Z. "Three-Month-Old Infants' Reactions to Simulated Maternal Depression." *Child Development,* 1983, *54,* 185–193.

Cortez, V. "Priming of Perceived Control in Young Children as a Buffer Against Fear-Inducing Events." Unpublished doctoral dissertation, Department of Psychology, University of California, Santa Barbara, 1991.

Cummings, E. M., and Cummings, J. L. "A Process-Oriented Approach to Children's Coping with Adults' Angry Behavior." *Developmental Review,* 1988, *8,* 296–321.

Ellis, H. C., Thomas, R. L., and Rodriguez, I. A. "Emotional Mood States and Memory: Elaborative Encoding, Semantic Processing, and Cognitive Effort." *Journal of Experimental Psychology: Learning, Memory, and Cognition,* 1984, *10,* 470–482.

El-Sheikh, M., Cummings, E. M., and Goetsch, V. L. "Coping with Adults' Angry Behavior: Behavioral, Physiological, and Verbal Responses in Preschoolers." *Developmental Psychology,* 1989, *25,* 490–498.

Gnepp, J., and Gould, M. E. "The Development of Personalized Inferences: Understanding of Other People's Emotional Reactions in Light of Their Prior Experience." *Child Development,* 1985, *56,* 1455–1464.

Hasher, L., and Zacks, R. T. "Automatic and Effortful Processes in Memory." *Journal of Experimental Psychology: General,* 1979, *108,* 356–388.

Hertel, P. T., and Narvaez, A. "Confusing Memories for Verbal and Nonverbal Communication." *Journal of Personality and Social Psychology,* 1986, *50,* 474–481.

Hoffman, M. L. "Empathy, Its Development, and Prosocial Implications." In C. Keasy (ed.), *Social Cognitive Development.* Nebraska Symposium on Motivation. Lincoln: University of Nebraska Press, 1977.

Hoffner, C., and Badzinski, D. M. "Children's Integration of Facial and Situational Cues to Emotion." *Child Development,* 1989, *60,* 411–422.

Howes, M. J., Hokanson, J. E., and Lowenstein, D. A. "Induction of Depressive Affect After Prolonged Exposure to a Mildly Depressed Individual." *Journal of Personality and Social Psychology,* 1985, *49,* 1110–1113.

Hsee, K., Hatfield, E., Carlson, J. G., and Chemtob, C. "The Effect of Power on Susceptibility to Emotional Contagion." *Cognition and Emotion,* 1990, *4,* 327–340.

Isen, A. M. "Toward Understanding the Role of Affect in Cognition." In W. Wyer and T. K. Srull (eds.), *Handbook of Social Cognition.* Vol. 13. Hillsdale, N.J.: Erlbaum, 1984.

Isen, A. M., and Daubman, K. A. "The Influence of Affect on Categorization." *Journal of Personality and Social Psychology,* 1984, *47,* 1206–1217.

Klinnert, M., Campos, J. J., Sorce, J., Emde, R., and Svejda, M. "Emotions as Behavior Regulators: Social Referencing in Infancy." In R. Plutchik and H. Kellerman (eds.), *Emotions in Early Development.* Vol. 2: *The Emotions.* San Diego, Calif.: Academic Press, 1983.

Lazarus, R. S., and Folkman, S. *Stress, Appraisal, and Coping.* New York: Springer, 1984.

Lefcourt, H. M., Miller, R. S., Ware, E. E., and Sherk, D. "Locus of Control as a Modifier of the Relationship Between Stressors and Moods." *Journal of Personality and Social Psychology,* 1981, *41,* 357–369.

Leight, K. A., and Ellis, H. C. "Emotional Mood States, Strategies, and State-Dependency in Memory." *Journal of Verbal Learning and Verbal Behavior,* 1981, *20,* 251–266.

Lelwica, M., and Haviland, J. M. "Response of Imitation: Ten-Week-Old Infants' Reactions to Three Emotion Expressions." Paper presented at the biennial meeting of the Society for Research in Child Development, Detroit, Michigan, April 1983.

Levenson, R. W., Ekman, P., and Friesen, W. V. "Voluntary Facial Action Generates Emotion-Specific Autonomic Nervous System Activity." *Psychophysiology,* 1990, *27,* 363–384.

Livesley, W. J., and Bromley, D. B. *Person Perception in Childhood and Adolescence.* New York: Wiley, 1973.

Phares, E. J. *Locus of Control in Personality.* Morristown, N.J.: General Learning Press, 1976.

Reichenbach, L., and Masters, J. C. "Children's Use of Expressive and Contextual Cues in Judgments of Emotion." *Child Development,* 1983, *54,* 993–1004.

Saarni, C. "Children's Understanding of Display Rules for Expressive Behavior." *Developmental Psychology,* 1979, *15,* 424–429.

Saarni, C. "An Observational Study of Children's Attempts to Monitor Their Expressive Behavior." *Child Development,* 1984, *55,* 1504–1513.

Sacks, C. H., and Bugental, D. B. "Attributions as Moderators of Affective and Behavioral Responses to Social Failure." *Journal of Personality and Social Psychology,* 1987, *53,* 939–947.

Sagi, A., and Hoffman, M. "Empathic Distress in the Newborn." *Developmental Psychology,* 1976, *12,* 175–176.

Schachter, S. *The Psychology of Affiliation.* Stanford, Calif.: Stanford University Press, 1959.

Shiffrin, R. M., and Schneider, W. "Controlled and Automatic Human Information Processing. Part 2: Perceptual Learning, Automatic Attending, and a General Theory." *Psychological Review,* 1977, *84,* 127–190.

Teasdale, J. D., and Fogarty, S. J. "Differential Effects of Induced Mood on Retrieval of Pleasant and Unpleasant Events from Episodic Memory." *Journal of Abnormal Psychology,* 1979, *88,* 248–257.

Vaughn, K. B., and Lanzetta, J. T. "Vicarious Instigation and Conditioning of Facial Expressive and Autonomic Responses to a Model's Expressive Display of Pain." *Journal of Personality and Social Psychology,* 1980, *36,* 909–923.

Zimbardo, P., and Formica, R. "Emotional Comparison and Self-Esteem as Determinants of Affiliation." *Journal of Personality,* 1963, *31,* 141–162.

DAPHNE BLUNT BUGENTAL is professor of social and developmental psychology at the University of California, Santa Barbara (UCSB).

VICTORIA CORTEZ is a doctoral candidate in developmental psychology at UCSB.

JAY BLUE is a lecturer at California State University, Chico.

Differences in social-cognitive development and children's ability to regulate their own emotional responses are implicated in developmental differences in children's strategies for influencing others' mood states.

Children's Emotional-Expressive Behaviors as Regulators of Others' Happy and Sad Emotional States

Carolyn Saarni

Systematic research on how children intentionally influence the emotional states of others is limited. Yet, as parents, we can generally recall instances where we have been the "targets" of our children's deliberate attempts to modify our emotional states or moods, such as when they try "to butter us up" so that we will capitulate to their desires or when they start to laugh as we irritably attempt to reproach them about some concern. Staying aggravated, much less maintaining a stern look, becomes very difficult indeed. Relevant research includes the myriad studies on prosocial behavior and empathy (see Eisenberg and Strayer, 1987a, for relevant reviews), which have documented that children as young as three or four years attempt to comfort distressed peers, apparently intentional efforts to intervene in the emotional states of others. Zahn-Waxler and Radke-

I thank Jane Weiskopf and Michael Crowley for their skillful assistance in conducting the videotaping for this study and for their help in coding the tapes. I also express my gratitude to Valerie Borg and Renee Soule for their sensitive interaction with the participating children; to the teachers and staff at Penngrove and Valley Vista elementary schools of the Petaluma School District, Sonoma County, California, for their helpful cooperation; and especially to the children for their enthusiastic involvement in this project.

This research was supported by a grant to the author by the National Science Foundation. Correspondence and requests for reprints may be sent to Carolyn Saarni, Department of Counseling, Sonoma State University, Rohnert Park, California 94928, USA.

Yarrow (1982) observed that even two-year-olds could initiate comforting or reparative behavior in another's behalf. Zahn-Waxler and Kochanska (1988) also have described preschoolers of depressed mothers displaying an unusual degree of appeasement behavior toward others. They propose that "this heightened sensitivity suggests the early learning of high levels of accountability in social interactions with others" (p. 227). This idea that some children may feel accountable for modifying another's emotional state is intriguing and may be related to some of the outcomes found in the research reported here.

Additional related research includes studies that focus on social-cognitive development. Using verbal reports, Covell and Abramovich (1987) found that children across the age span of five to fifteen years believed that they could affect their mothers' emotional states (especially in provoking their anger). Dunn (1988) also describes children's attempts to influence the emotions of others from the standpoint of their social-cognitive development. Finally, Carlson, Felleman, and Masters (1983) and McCoy and Masters (1985) also investigated children's verbal reports on how to intervene in another's emotional state. Carlson, Felleman, and Masters found that four- and five-year-old children were willing to help alter the negative feelings of a story protagonist, and McCoy and Masters found that five- to twelve-year-old subjects were able to nominate intervention strategies for changing the emotional states of story protagonists. In the latter research, the youngest children were more likely to suggest material nurturant strategies, such as giving candy, in order to alleviate someone's sadness. Older children were more likely to nominate social interventions in order to modify others' feelings.

An Observational Study of Children's Emotional-Expressive Behavior

The rationale for the present observational study was in part derived from (1) the McCoy and Masters (1985) study, since I was interested in the sorts of social interventions older children would demonstrate when asked to help cheer up an ostensibly sad adult, and if there was no candy available, how younger children would try to ameliorate another's distress; (2) the research summarized by Zahn-Waxler and Kochanska (1988), wherein children responded in ways suggesting a felt sense of responsibility for others' feelings; and (3) my own prior observational research on children's attempts to monitor their expressive behavior with a (confederate) gift giver from whom they received a disappointing gift after having previously received candy and money from her (Saarni, 1984).

With the present sample of school-age children, I manipulated their expectations for a second pleasant interaction with a "market researcher" with whom they had interacted the week before in a positive way. At the end of that first meeting, each child received a set of T-shirt decorating crayons for participating in the "market research." Upon returning for their second meeting, however, they were faced with a request by a second research assistant to help cheer up the market researcher, who was now sad. The assistant also assured the children that they would get their crayons regardless of whether they were successful in their efforts to help.

The theoretical links among ability to influence another's emotional state, self-regulation, and social competence should be made explicit here. Elsewhere I have defined *emotional competence* as the demonstration of self-efficacy in the context of emotion-eliciting social transactions (Saarni, 1988). It is this quality of self-efficacy, which is the skill to obtain the outcomes that one desires, that is embedded in the ability to regulate one's own experience of emotional arousal in a way that is adaptive and functional for oneself (Thompson, 1988). If we are faced with having to interact with an individual whose emotional state may provoke our own emotional arousal (in short, an emotion-eliciting social transaction), how do we respond in an adaptive fashion? The response of becoming overwhelmed by another's emotional state is not likely to be adaptive, nor is completely ignoring or distorting the emotional situation. But the ability to self-regulate our own emotional responses in a way that allows us to cope is generally adaptive, and this coping is where social competence comes into play: The social skills and cognitive capabilities that we have developed up to that point become relevant to how we go about coping in the social encounter. If we know that some strategies are more effective than others when faced with the prospect, for example, of having to cheer up a sad person, and if we have been able effectively to regulate our own emotional arousal to the sad person's display, then we are in a considerably better position of influencing for the better the mood state of the sad person.

In sum, this quasi-naturalistic study provides a taxonomy of emotional-expressive behaviors used by school-age children (seven to twelve years of age) in an interaction with a happy researcher—the comparative baseline data—and again in a second interaction with the same researcher who then displayed sadness. However, prior to this second encounter, the children agreed to try to ameliorate the sad mood state of the experimenter; thus, this manipulation introduced the element of intentional influence on another's emotional state. The repertoire of emotional-expressive behaviors that was coded was broad, ranging from facial gestures to degree of task compliance and verbal elaboration. I anticipated that the older children, compared to the younger, would use more positively toned expressive behaviors (for example, smiles, variable vocal intonation, natural eye-contact patterns) in their attempts to alleviate the sad mood of the market researcher. The younger children, lacking any concrete means with which to comfort the researcher, would presumably be more at a loss as to what to do. I expected that they would show more anxiety or tension-related expressive behaviors. I also expected to find gender differences, such as girls exhibiting more smiles than shown by the boys in their interaction with the market researcher, a pattern that has been found in several observational investigations on expressive behavior (Cole, 1986; Saarni, 1984). The investigation included a phenomenological element as well since the confederates monitored their own emotional reactions to their meetings with the children.

Method

Thus, the present observational study provides data that shed light both on the social-emotional strategies that children are likely to employ and on whether they are able to regulate their own arousal so as to effectively influence the sad mood state of their interactant without becoming overly susceptible to emotional contagion (see Hsee, Hatfield, Carlson, and Chemtob, 1990) or becoming overwhelmed by the other's distress.

Sample. Eighty children in three age groups participated: second graders (fourteen girls and twenty boys, mean age of 7.9 years), fourth graders (eight girls and fifteen boys, mean age of 9 years), and sixth graders (thirteen girls and ten boys, mean age of 11.6 years). All had parental permission to participate, and the parents were fully informed about the nature of the deceptive research methods. The socioeconomic status of the families ranged from lower-middle to upper-middle class; the majority were Caucasian, and all children were proficient in speaking English. All of the children were residents of a small Northern California city and attended public school.

Session 1: Happy Interaction. Two pairs of research assistants met with the children individually; each pair consisted of the "market researcher" and another who was ostensibly her assistant. The assistant took the children from their classrooms to another small room in the school where the market researcher was waiting. One-by-one, each child was then seated across a small table from the market researcher. Behind the child, a full-length mirror was positioned in such a way as to permit simultaneous videotaping of the child and of the market researcher's reflection while interacting with the child. The assistant managed the video camera during the interaction.

In this first session, the market researcher introduced herself and engaged the child in a warm and friendly manner. She then introduced the market research task, which consisted of a set of vivid magazine pictures without any text, from which the child was to select those pictures he or she thought could be used in children's books. Throughout this part of the meeting the market researcher continued to demonstrate a lively and responsive interest in the child. After three minutes the assistant gave a signal that the time was up, and the market researcher concluded the session on a friendly note and indicated that the two of them would meet again in a week. The assistant returned the child to his or her classroom and during the walk back asked the child about the meeting with the market researcher (the exit interview). Meanwhile, the market researcher filled out her subjective report on her interaction with the child.

Session 2: Sad Interaction. A week later the same assistant retrieved the child subject from her or his classroom to meet again with the market researcher. However, while walking to the videotaping room, the assistant said the following scripted remarks to the child: "Listen, maybe you could help me. The person who is working with me is feeling really sort of down, like sad, today. I feel badly seeing her this way; if you think you can, maybe try to cheer her up a bit. I have to work with her all morning, and maybe together we can help her feel a bit happier. Do you think you could help me with that?" The assistant also assured the child that he or she would afterward receive a gift for helping with the project.

The market researcher in this sad session did not turn around to greet the child until he or she was seated. She maintained a solemn expression and introduced a second set of pictures to the child. During this exchange and the subsequent selection of pictures, the market researcher had eye contact with the child but did not lean forward, avoided smiling, and minimized talking. Overall, the women's posture was dispirited, slumped, and with little movement, if any.

After the assistant again gave the three-minute termination signal, it was expected that some children might then finally try to say something to cheer up the market researcher. Any such effort was to be allowed to unfold naturally, and the market researcher was at that time to smile back at the child. If the child made no further overture and looked quite ready to leave the room, the market researcher was to show some visible, expressive improvement in mood. All children received a positive departure comment from a now smiling market researcher. This closing of the session on a positive note with the children was considered ethically necessary, especially since the children had been coaxed into helping to cheer up the market researcher.

As the assistant walked the child back to her or his classroom, the second exit interview was conducted, and during this time the market researcher filled out another subjective report form on her interaction with the child.

Exit Interviews. Exit interviews were used with the children and were intended to serve as both a comprehension and manipulation check following the happy and sad sessions.

Happy Session. The following questions were posed to the children upon returning to their classrooms: (1) (comprehension check) "How do you think Renee [or Valerie] was feeling today?" (2) "How could you tell that?" (3) "Did you like doing this project or was it just sort of OK?" (4) "Why?"

Sad Session. The following questions and probes were asked after the second meeting: (1) (comprehension check) "How do you think Renee [or Valerie] was feeling today?" (2) "How could you tell?" If the child said something such as "sad" or "bad" to the first question, and they could tell because the assistant had told them so, they were asked, "What else seemed to show you how she felt?" (3) "Do you think you were able to cheer her up a bit?" (4) "What do you think you did to help cheer her up?" The children then received their gifts for participating in the project.

Subjective Reports. To assess how the researchers felt after the happy and sad sessions, their subjective reports of mood states were obtained. This procedure allowed me to examine if children's efforts affected the researchers.

Happy Session. The market researcher responded to the following questions for each child: (1) "Do you feel the child responded positively to you in this first session?" (2) "If yes, was your impression based on any of the following? Check as many as apply: child smiled easily, child verbalized readily, child made eye contact appropriately, child showed increasing relaxation and 'warming up' as the session progressed." (3) "How comfortable do you think the child was in this situation?" (A 1–4 scale was used, ranging from very uncomfortable to very comfortable.) (4) "How did you feel with this child?" (A 1–5 scale was used, ranging from uncomfortable to feeling very positively about the interaction.)

Sad Session. After acting in a sad or depressed fashion with each child, the market researcher again rated her impressions for each child: (1) "In comparison to your first meeting with this child, do you feel that the child's response to you was affected by your despondency?" (2) "If yes, was your impression based on any of the following? Check as many as apply: child avoided eye contact as much as possible, child did not smile, child appeared intimidated by my mood state, child appeared withdrawn or despondent herself/himself, child did not talk much and performed the task perfunctorily, child appeared to ignore my changed mood state, child exhibited exaggerated and somewhat phony-looking cheerful behavior, child addressed my change in mood state and made an appropriate gesture." (3) "How comfortable do you think the child was in this situation?" (A 1–4 scale was used, ranging from very uncomfortable to very comfortable.) (4) "How sorely were you tempted to smile *as a result of the child's overtures* and/or emotional cues for you to cheer up?" (A 1–3 scale was used, ranging from not much to quite a bit.) (5) "How did you feel with this child?" (A 1–4 scale was used, ranging from guilty feeling to relieved.)

We conducted an extensive debriefing with the children after data collection had been completed in each classroom.

Coding. The videotapes were coded according to a scheme that was empirically developed by myself and two experienced graduate students. We rejected the microlevel coding of systems such as Friesen and Ekman's

(1984) emotional facial action coding system (EMFACS) and Izard's (1979) maximally discriminative facial movement coding system (MAX) because we were not solely interested in facial expressions of prototypical emotions. In addition, Camras and others (1988) compared global ratings of posed emotion with EMFACS coding; the two scoring systems were only moderately correlated in that EMFACS did not appear to be as sensitive to as many of the posed emotions as were the naive raters. My position here is that measurement schemes need to be both readily useable as well as reliable in their application if we are to make sense of subjects' emotional-expressive behavior. Thus, our approach was to adapt and elaborate the relatively simple and straightforward coding system that I had used in my earlier observational study (Saarni, 1984). The elaborations included several global ratings of behaviors such as task compliance (for example, how eagerly or carefully the children were in selecting the pictures), degree of appropriate eye contact, and talkativeness. Additional behaviors were also included that described hand and body movements, especially those that seemed particularly noticeable in the videotapes or that matched movements mentioned by investigators of nonverbal behavior (see Harper, Wiens, and Matarazzo, 1978; Scherer and Ekman, 1982). Exhibit 6.1 contains the full observational coding scheme for this project according to a priori aggregates (see below for explanation).

Exhibit 6.1. Observational Coding Scheme for Both Happy and Sad Sessions, Grouped According to Social-Emotional Aggregates

Positive Aggregate
  Relaxed, broad smile (teeth show or lips parted)
  Appropriateness of eye contact (ratings 3, 4, or 5 on ordinal scale)
  Raised eyebrows
  Uses expressive hand gestures while talking
  Leans forward
  Giggles or laughs
  Gets "market researcher" to laugh or smile in response to child
  Variable pitch and vocal expressiveness
  Variable loudness of voice
  Degree of elaboration in justifying pictures chosen (ratings 3 and 4)
  Quality of talk across session (ratings 3 and 4)
  Overall compliance with task (ratings 3 and 4)

Social Monitoring Aggregate
  Abrupt onset/offset of smile
  Rapid glances at market researcher when neither is speaking
  Delays departure from room, despite cues
  Slight or closed lip smile
  Staring at market researcher
  Tilts head

Exhibit 6.1 *(continued)*

Tension/Anxiety Aggregate
Pressing, pursing, biting, or sucking of lips
Bites or mouths clothing
Cheek puffing
Prolonged tongue protrusions
Jaw wiggling, rotating, thrusting, and so on
Nose wrinkle
Rapid, nervous blinking
Looking around room or at ceiling in a scanning fashion
Face/nose touching or scratching
Finger(s) in mouth, on lips, or nail biting
Touches/scratches hair, scalp, ears, and so on
Touches/scratches upper or lower torso
Hides hands in pockets/sleeves, sits on hands, and so on
Rubs eyes
Finger rubbing/scratching
Holds/folds hands or arms together
Hand wringing or twisting
Covers face or part of face with hands
Holds picture in front of face
Hand fidgeting or drumming (with pictures, table, chair, and so on)
Stands up (during session)
Shrugs
Twisting and shifting in chair
Leans on table
Puts knees against table edge
Pumps up/down in seat
Stretching

Negative Aggregate
Tense, square-looking smile (lips open and teeth showing)
Down-turned mouth (as in a frown or grimace)
Appropriateness of eye contact (ratings 1 and 2)
Knits eyebrows
Leans backward
Bolts from room at end of session
Sharp breath exhalation, snorting, grumping, or groaning
Sighing
Monotone most of the session
Very soft voice most of the session
Degree of elaboration in justifying pictures chosen (ratings 1 and 2)
Quality of talk across session (ratings 1 and 2)
Overall compliance with task (ratings 1 and 2)

Two graduate research assistants were trained by me to code the videotapes, using the observational categories in Exhibit 6.1 for both the happy and sad sessions. In order to assess interrater reliability, videotapes from both the happy and the sad sessions were randomly selected for twenty children, representing each grade level and both boys and girls. These tapes were independently coded by the two research assistants. They achieved 76.8 percent complete agreement, averaged across all categories listed in Exhibit 6.1 and both sessions (forty tapes were coded in total: twenty children by two sessions each). Using the slightly more relaxed criterion of whether or not the two coders were within one point of each other on any category, they then achieved 91.7 percent agreement.

The coding categories were grouped a priori into four meaningful aggregates: (1) positive behaviors (twelve categories), (2) social monitoring behaviors (six categories), (3) tension or anxiety behaviors (twenty-seven categories), and (4) negative behaviors (thirteen categories). Thus, an aggregate score consisted of the frequency of behaviors coded according to its respective categories. These aggregates should not be viewed as emotion aggregates (obviously, social monitoring is not an emotion); rather, the aggregates are characterized by what is conveyed in emotionally toned social transactions. The justifications for assigning a particular observational category to a particular aggregate were based on conclusions drawn from the research literature on nonverbal communication (for example, Harper, Wiens, and Matarazzo, 1978; Mehrabian, 1972). However, a qualification is warranted because that literature is largely based on adults: The social psychological meaning of some nonverbal behaviors may not necessarily be the same for school-age children. It should also be noted that all aggregates are mutually exclusive in terms of how they are constituted; however, those individual observational categories that required an ordinal scale rating (such as degree of verbal elaboration, appropriateness of eye contact) had their ratings dichotomized, and high and low ratings were then assigned either to the positive or to the negative aggregates.

Results

I first compare data for the happy and sad sessions. This is followed by more in-depth analyses within each session.

Comparison of Happy and Sad Sessions: Repeated-Measures Analyses. Only the aggregate scores were used in the age group-by-sex-by-session, repeated-measures analyses of variance. For the positive behavior aggregate, the repeated measure—session—was highly significant ($F[1,74]$ = 21.90, $p < .001$); all age groups showed declines in their mean frequency of positive emotional-expressive behavior when interacting with the "sad" market researcher, despite being asked to try to cheer her up.

For the social monitoring aggregate, the interaction of age group by session missed significance ($p < .08$), but the trends here were that the youngest children proportionately showed the greatest increase in their mean frequency of social monitoring behaviors, and the boys in the two oldest age groups decreased their social monitoring behaviors.

For the tension/anxiety aggregate, the repeated measure of session was again significant ($F[1,74] = 10.24, p < .002$), as was the interaction of session by age ($F[2,74] = 5.32, p < .007$). This interaction was due to the fourth graders' maintenance of their moderate level of tension behaviors from the happy session to the sad session, and the sixth graders' substantial increase (about 50 percent) in their mean frequency of tension behaviors in the sad session. The second graders' mean frequency of tension behaviors in the sad session also increased over their happy session level, but only by about 15 percent.

For the final aggregate, negative emotional-expressive behaviors, the repeated measure of session was again highly significant ($F[1,74] = 20.34, p < .001$). However, no interactions were significant, and all age groups showed increases in their mean frequency of negative behaviors in the sad session, with gains ranging from 30 percent (fourth graders) to 50 percent (sixth graders). Given this pattern of significant effects for session, I turn now to more fine-grained analyses of the happy and the sad sessions.

Happy Session. For the happy session, the influence of the market researcher, developmental differences, exit interviews, and subjective reports are now examined.

Influence of "Market Researcher." We examined the possible effect of market researcher in the second- and fourth-grade data. (Due to administrative constraints, only one market researcher, hereafter referred to as B, conducted all interviews with the sixth graders; therefore, the effect of market researcher could be examined only in the two youngest age groups.) The effect was significant for the positive aggregate ($F[1,50] = 15.67, p < .001$), with B generally eliciting more positive behaviors in the happy session than did A (analyses of individual expressive behaviors indicated that B elicited significantly more relaxed smiles). The effect of market researcher was also significant for the tension/anxiety aggregate ($F[1,50] = 5.26, p < .03$), with A generally eliciting more tension/anxiety behaviors during the happy session with these two youngest age groups than did B (analyses of selected tension behaviors indicated that A elicited significantly more biting of lips). These outcomes bear an interesting reciprocal relationship to how the market researchers themselves felt, as recorded in their subjective reports.

Developmental Differences Observed. The only significant age effect for the aggregate scores in the happy session was that the oldest children significantly produced more positive behaviors than did the other two age groups ($F[2,74] = 18.94, p < .001$; M's = 11.21, 8.13, and 19.35 for the second, fourth, and sixth graders, respectively). I next looked at age differences for several of the observational categories that most frequently contributed to the positive aggregate: number of instances of relaxed smiles, raised eyebrows, and getting the market researcher to smile. Significant age group effects occurred for each of these observational categories, and they all favored the oldest children (p's < .001–.004). An age group-by-sex interaction just missed significance for getting the market researcher to smile (p < .06): The oldest boys were the most successful in eliciting reciprocated smiles. Across age groups, the boys also significantly raised their eyebrows more during the happy session than girls, and, although not significant, the oldest boys did this more than twice as often as any other age-by-sex subgroup. (Perhaps when the preadolescent boys raised their eyebrows, the market researcher was more likely to smile back at them.) I also examined the slight smile category for age and sex effects (this category was included in the social monitoring aggregate, but I think this may be an ambiguous assignment for children). Age was again significant $(F[2,74] = 30.92, p < .001)$, with the oldest children again showing this expressive behavior two to four times as often as the two youngest age groups (M's = 1.26, 2.26, and 5.04 for the second, fourth, and sixth graders, respectively). However, a caveat is in order here: Since B was the sole interviewer with the oldest children, the significant results reported above may reflect the dynamics of their interaction together more than developmental differences.

Exit Interview Results. Chi-square analyses were used to evaluate the outcomes of the exit interviews. No age group or gender effects occurred in that very large majorities of all age groups believed that the market researcher was happy or in a good mood, and they could tell how she felt by the way she looked ("she looked happy" or "she was smiling"). The majority also thought that the task was fun and gave credible rationales for why they liked it.

Subjective Reports. Chi-square analyses were again used to examine the individual responses. The market researchers' ratings also indicated that a large majority of the children were thought to respond positively to the interaction. On the "comfort" scale, the market researchers rated the middle age group as somewhat more uncomfortable than were the youngest and oldest groups. The only significant effect, however, was for the comfort level of the market researcher as she evaluated her feelings about interacting with the children $(\chi^2[8] = 16.20, p < .04)$. Thirty-five percent of the second graders and 52 percent of the sixth graders received the most positive evaluations, whereas only 13 percent of the fourth graders were perceived this way. These self-ratings of researcher comfort in working with the children dovetail nicely with the researchers' perceptions of the fourth graders as less comfortable than the other two age groups.

An examination of the subjective reports with the responses coded, as though they were continuous data, permitted the inclusion of the effect of market researcher. These analyses revealed only a single significant effect, which was for the felt comfort of the market researcher when interacting with the children ($F[1,40] = 5.33$, $p < .03$). Researcher A felt less comfortable ($M = 3.05$) than B ($M = 3.82$), but recall that this finding was based only on a comparison of the two youngest age groups because B conducted all of the meetings with the sixth-grade children. Conceivably, A's lower comfort level with the children in this first happy session influenced their reciprocal responses to her, namely, their increased tension behaviors and their somewhat reduced positive behaviors.

Sad Session. For the sad session, the influence of the market researcher, developmental differences, exit interviews, and subjective reports are now examined.

Influence of "Market Researcher." Age group-by-sex-by-experimenter analyses of variance were calculated to examine the effect of the two market researchers on the aggregate scores. There were no significant effects.

Developmental Differences Observed. Significant age effects were found for the positive aggregate ($F[2,74] = 20.49$, $p < .001$) and for the tension/anxiety aggregate ($F[2,74] = 4.65$, $p < .01$). The oldest children again showed considerably more positive behaviors in the sad session than did the two youngest age groups (M's = 7.65, 6.00, and 17.00 for the second, fourth, and sixth graders, respectively). The middle age group, the fourth graders, appeared to be the source of the significant age effect on the tension/anxiety aggregate in that they expressed fewer anxiety behaviors (M's = 14.74, 9.87, and 15.57 for the second, fourth, and sixth graders, respectively).

In examining several of the individual expressive behavior categories that were thought likely to have contributed to these significant age differences in the aggregated scores, we found significant age differences ($p < .001$) for frequency of relaxed smiles, raised eyebrows, and slight smiles (from the social monitoring aggregate), all favoring the oldest children (relaxed smile, M's = .71, .09, and 3.09; raised eyebrows, M's = 1.41, 1.00, and 3.17; slight smile, M's = .97, 1.13, and 3.10; for the second, fourth, and sixth graders, respectively). Gender missed being significant ($p < .10$) for frequency of relaxed smiles; however, the girls' mean was about 50 percent higher than the boys' (1.54 versus .96, respectively). There were no significant or near-significant age-by-sex interactions.

In examining a number of the individual behaviors that most frequently contributed to the tension/anxiety aggregate, we found that age group was significant for only two behaviors: finger rubbing and scratching ($p < .05$) and folding one's arms or clasping one's hands together ($p < .04$). For both categories, the oldest children evidenced a higher frequency than shown by the two youngest age groups (finger rubbing/scratching, M's = .38, .57, and 1.48; folding arms/hands, M's = .94, .52, and 1.57; for second, fourth, and sixth graders, respectively). This breakdown did not illuminate which anxious behaviors the fourth graders were doing less of, relative to the two other age groups, given that their mean aggregate score was the lowest. If anything, these two significant age effects suggest that the oldest children, while smiling considerably more than did the younger children, were also fidgeting with their arms and hands more during the sad session.

Exit Interview Results. Chi-square analyses were used to evaluate the children's responses to the exit interview questions. Again, the vast majority of children across age groups and gender correctly perceived that the market researcher was feeling sad, or gave an equivalent word or phrase, and said that they could tell how she was feeling by how she looked or acted. A significant age effect was obtained for their responses to the question about whether they thought that they had been able to cheer her up ($\chi^2[4] = 10.37$, $p < .03$). This age effect was due to the much lower proportion of fourth graders who believed that they had been successful in cheering her up (77, 39, and 74 percent for the second, fourth, and sixth graders, respectively). When asked what they thought that they had done to cheer up the market researcher, significant age differences were not found; however, from a descriptive standpoint, the two youngest age groups had about three times as many "don't know" responses as the oldest children, who, in turn, gave more social and interpersonal rationales (47 percent of their responses, which included comments such as "I tried to talk about pleasant things" and "I tried to be very nice to her"), or explicitly commented on their own emotional-expressive behavior as a way to cheer her up (24 percent of the sixth graders' responses were of this type, typically taking the verbal form "I smiled at her a lot"). The fourth graders had the highest proportion of rationales that focused on their performances on the picture selection task as their means of trying to cheer up the market researcher (31 percent of their responses fell into this category, for example, "I told her which pictures were the good ones"). While not significant, girls gave twice as many responses as did the boys that were coded as rationales emphasizing their own expressive behavior as their means for cheering up the market researcher (recall that their mean number of relaxed smiles was about 50 percent higher).

Subjective Reports. Virtually all of the children were rated by the market researchers as responsive to their depressed mood state. A significant age group effect was found for the comfort level of the child ($\chi^2[4] = 20.07$, $p < .0005$), with 47 percent of the youngest children being perceived by the market researchers as very uncomfortable, compared to 26 percent of the fourth graders and none of the sixth graders. Fully half of the sixth-grade children were rated by the market researchers as somewhat comfortable. The comfort level of the market researchers was also significant relative to age group ($\chi^2[6] = 14.28$, $p < .03$), with the researchers feeling more often relieved when interacting with the sixth graders (55 percent) and more often feeling guilty when working with the second graders (49 percent).

Conversion of the ratings to continuous data permitted examination of the influence of market researcher on the subjective reports for the two youngest age groups. The influence proved to be significant for comfort of child ($F[1,50] = 9.63$, $p < .003$), with A perceiving the children as more uncomfortable than did B. The interactions of age group and sex with market researcher were also significant ($p < .03$ and .01, respectively), with A perceiving the youngest children as more uncomfortable than did B and also perceiving the boys as more uncomfortable than did B. The market researcher's comfort was also significantly influenced by who was doing the report ($F[1,50] = 6.55$, $p < .01$): A also felt worse than did B.

Discussion and Conclusion

The results of this study point toward the important role played by individual differences when a child is faced with an interaction in which the other displays a negative emotional state. Differences in social-cognitive development and ability to regulate one's own emotional response were clearly implicated in the developmental differences found. However, within each age group, there was still a considerable range of emotional responses to the request to cheer up the sad market researcher. Although some of this variability may be due to the influence of the two different market researchers used for the two youngest age groups, even when the repeated-measures analyses were calculated with only B's data (recall that B met with all three age groups), the pattern of significant effects for session in the positive, negative, and tension/anxiety aggregates remained the same (p's $< .001$). Within each age group, those children who seemed most uncomfortable may have been those who were somewhat less mature relative to their age mates in their ability to regulate their own emotional states and to distinguish them from those of others (see Thompson, 1988). Thus, perhaps they were "engulfed" by the sad market researcher's despondency and manifested emotional responses that looked as though they were feeling personal distress about her emotional state (Eisenberg and Strayer, 1987b). Other individual differences may have to do with the degree to which children have to deal with chronic negative emotions in their families. Recall Zahn-Waxler and Kochanska's (1988, p. 227) earlier quoted comments on how some children—typically, those from homes with depressed parents—seem too ready to feel accountable for others' emotional experiences. Although the relevance of these observations to the present study is not verifiable, such children in the present study may have displayed distress during the sad session because of their felt sense of obligation to ameliorate the sadness of the market researcher. Yet, they had to operate within a causal vacuum as to what had caused her despondency.

Several possible explanations may account for the behavior of the nine- and ten-year-olds (fourth graders), who were rather flat in their emotional expressiveness in both sessions relative to the seven- and eight-year-olds (second graders) and to the eleven- and twelve-year-olds (sixth graders). There are at least three possible explanations of this finding. One is simply variation in sampling; the second is the different influences of the two market researchers; and the third is the developmental social and emotional tasks of the latency-age children as opposed to the youngest and oldest groups of children. I lean toward this third possible interpretation: The emotional expressiveness of the youngest children was influenced in part by their discomfort at having to meet with a stranger outside of their familiar classroom for the happy session and by their distress at having to try to influence her sad mood state in the sad session. The oldest children's expressive behavior was simultaneously much more positive in tone as well as anxious. Conceivably, their more mature social cognition provoked more self-evaluation about their efficacy in cheering up the sad market re-searcher, or provoked their exasperation with her decline into depression given their pleasurable exchange with her the week before. The result was higher ratings for finger rubbing/scratching and hand/arm folding or clasp-ing and increased negative behavior. Meanwhile, the fourth graders were instrumentally oriented and somewhat avoidant of emotion in general, and their replies to the exit interview after the sad session are illuminating: They focused most on task performance, and they thought that the way to make someone feel better was essentially to be a good boy or girl by doing the job well. This sample of nine-year-olds appeared to be occupied with learning the instrumental routines of our culture, and some of those rou-tines include separating one's own emotional responses from those of another (Thompson, 1988). Perhaps in learning that emotional coping routine, children go a bit overboard at first in adopting a degree of *emo-tional disconnection,* which describes the minimally emotionally responsive behavior of the nine-year-olds in my sample.

In conclusion, this research suggests ways to investigate how children come to regulate their own emotional experience in conjunction with their attempts to respond competently in interpersonal transactions. Processes of social control as well as self-efficacy were involved in this quasi-natural-istic study; the large role played by individual differences was clearly man-ifested in the children's emotional-expressive displays and in their responses to the exit interviews after the sad sessions. The inclusion of the market researchers' subjective self-reports also proved useful in accounting for some of the differences among the children in their emotional-expres-sive responses to the market researchers.

References

Camras, L., Ribordy, S., Hill, J., Martino, S., Spaccarelli, S., and Stefani, R. "Recognition and Posing of Emotional Expressions by Abused Children and Their Mothers." *Developmental Psychology,* 1988, *24,* 776–781.

Carlson, C., Felleman, E., and Masters, J. C. "Influence of Children's Emotional States on the Recognition of Emotion in Peer and Social Motives to Change Another's Emotional State." *Motivation and Emotion*, 1983, 7, 61–79.

Cole, P. M. "Children's Spontaneous Control of Facial Expressions." *Child Development*, 1986, 57, 1309–1321.

Covell, K., and Abramovitch, R. "Understanding Emotion in the Family: Children's and Parents' Attributions of Happiness, Sadness, and Anger." *Child Development*, 1987, 58, 985–991.

Dunn, J. *The Beginnings of Social Understanding.* Oxford, England: Basil Blackwell, 1988.

Eisenberg, N., and Strayer, J. (eds.). *Empathy and Its Development.* New York: Cambridge University Press, 1987a.

Eisenberg, N., and Strayer, J. "Critical Issues in the Study of Empathy." In N. Eisenberg and J. Strayer (eds.), *Empathy and Its Development.* New York: Cambridge University Press, 1987b.

Friesen, W. V., and Ekman, P. *EMFACS: Emotion Facial Action Coding System.* San Francisco: Department of Psychiatry, University of California, 1984.

Harper, R., Wiens, A., and Matarazzo, J. *Nonverbal Communication: The State of the Art.* New York: Wiley, 1978.

Hsee, K., Hatfield, E., Carlson, J. G., and Chemtob, C. "The Effect of Power on Susceptibility to Emotional Contagion." *Cognition and Emotion*, 1990, 4, 327–340.

Izard, C. *The Maximally Descriminative Facial Movement Coding System.* Newark: Instructional Resources Center, University of Delaware, 1979.

McCoy, C., and Masters, J. C. "The Development of Children's Strategies for the Social Control of Emotion." *Child Development*, 1985, 56, 1214–1222.

Mehrabian, A. *Nonverbal Communication.* Hawthorne, N.Y.: Aldine, 1972.

Saarni, C. "An Observational Study of Children's Attempts to Monitor Their Expressive Behavior." *Child Development*, 1984, 55, 1504–1513.

Saarni, C. "Emotional Competence: How Emotions and Relationships Become Integrated." In R. A. Thompson (ed.), *Socioemotional Development.* Nebraska Symposium on Motivation, vol. 36. Lincoln: University of Nebraska Press, 1988.

Scherer, K., and Ekman, P. (eds.). *Handbook of Methods in Nonverbal Behavior Research.* New York: Cambridge University Press, 1982.

Thompson, R. A. "Emotion and Self-Regulation." In R. A. Thompson (ed.), *Socioemotional Development.* Nebraska Symposium on Motivation, vol. 36. Lincoln: University of Nebraska Press, 1988.

Zahn-Waxler, C., and Kochanska, G. "The Origins of Guilt." In R. A. Thompson (ed.), *Socioemotional Development.* Nebraska Symposium on Motivation, vol. 36. Lincoln: University of Nebraska Press, 1988.

Zahn-Waxler, C., and Radke-Yarrow, M. "The Development of Altruism: Alternative Research Strategies." In N. Eisenberg (ed.), *The Development of Prosocial Behavior.* San Diego, Calif.: Academic Press, 1982.

CAROLYN SAARNI is professor of counseling, Sonoma State University, California.

INDEX

ORDERING INFORMATION

NEW DIRECTIONS FOR CHILD DEVELOPMENT is a series of paperback books that presents the latest research findings on all aspects of children's psychological development, including their cognitive, social, moral, and emotional growth. Books in the series are published quarterly in Fall, Winter, Spring, and Summer and are available for purchase by subscription as well as by single copy.

SUBSCRIPTIONS for 1992 cost $52.00 for individuals (a savings of 20 percent over single-copy prices) and $70.00 for institutions, agencies, and libraries. Please do not send institutional checks for personal subscriptions. Standing orders are accepted.

SINGLE COPIES cost $17.95 when payment accompanies order. (California, New Jersey, New York, and Washington, D.C., residents please include appropriate sales tax.) Billed orders will be charged postage and handling.

DISCOUNTS FOR QUANTITY ORDERS are available. Please write to the address below for information.

ALL ORDERS must include either the name of an individual or an official purchase order number. Please submit your order as follows:
   Subscriptions: specify series and year subscription is to begin
   Single copies: include individual title code (such as CD1)

MAIL ALL ORDERS TO:
   Jossey-Bass Publishers
   350 Sansome Street
   San Francisco, California 94104

FOR SALES OUTSIDE OF THE UNITED STATES CONTACT:
   Maxwell Macmillan International Publishing Group
   866 Third Avenue
   New York, New York 10022